Design Patterns in PHP and Laravel

■ ■ ■

Kelt Dockins

Apress®

Design Patterns in PHP and Laravel

Kelt Dockins
Dolph, Arkansas
USA

ISBN-13 (pbk): 978-1-4842-2450-2   ISBN-13 (electronic): 978-1-4842-2451-9
DOI 10.1007/978-1-4842-2451-9

Library of Congress Control Number: 2016961807

Managing Director: Welmoed Spahr
Acquisitions Editor: Louise Corrigan
Technical Reviewer: Martin Bean
Editorial Board: Steve Anglin, Pramila Balan, Laura Berendson, Aaron Black, Louise Corrigan,
    Jonathan Gennick, Todd Green, Robert Hutchinson, Celestin Suresh John, Nikhil Karkal,
    James Markham, Susan McDermott, Matthew Moodie, Natalie Pao, Gwenan Spearing
Coordinating Editor: Nancy Chen
Copy Editor: Mary Behr
Compositor: SPi Global
Indexer: SPi Global
Artist: SPi Global

Distributed to the book trade worldwide by Springer Science+Business Media New York,
233 Spring Street, 6th Floor, New York, NY 10013. Phone 1-800-SPRINGER, fax (201) 348-4505, e-mail orders-ny@springer-sbm.com, or visit www.springer.com. Apress Media, LLC is a California LLC and the sole member (owner) is Springer Science + Business Media Finance Inc (SSBM Finance Inc). SSBM Finance Inc is a **Delaware** corporation.

For information on translations, please e-mail rights@apress.com, or visit www.apress.com.

Apress and friends of ED books may be purchased in bulk for academic, corporate, or promotional use. eBook versions and licenses are also available for most titles. For more information, reference our Special Bulk Sales–eBook Licensing web page at www.apress.com/bulk-sales.

Any source code or other supplementary materials referenced by the author in this text are available to readers at www.apress.com. For detailed information about how to locate your book's source code, go to www.apress.com/source-code/. Readers can also access source code at SpringerLink in the Supplementary Material section for each chapter.

Printed on acid-free paper

Contents at a Glance

Contents

About the Author

Kelt Dockins is a humble narcissistic web developer. He works as a full stack freelancer. He specializes in quick-to-market web applications and minimum viable products for start-ups. He has worked on small projects, medium-size projects, and even a few small-medium-sized projects. He loves being a father, a husband, and a developer. He's worked with many programming languages such as Visual Basic 6.0, C++, Java, Perl, bash, prolog, .NET stack, HTML, CSS, JavaScript and PHP. For the last three years, he's been using PHP and the ever-so-popular Laravel framework to stay at home and eat bacon while earning it at the same time. He does love bacon.

About the Technical Reviewer

Martin Bean is an experienced full-stack developer, specializing in PHP and related technologies. Based in Newcastle upon Tyne, UK, he is currently team lead on a Laravel-based product, a position he took after running his own consultancy business for nearly five years.

He is also very active in the web development community. He tweets regularly as @martinbean, maintains his own blog at martinbean.co.uk, and is also co-organizer of his local PHP and Laravel user groups.

Introduction

Hello there. I see you've met a few characters that will be in this book. Don't worry; there will be plenty more where that came from!

Please allow me to introduce myself. I'm Kelt. Together we are going to explore design patterns together. Not only that, but we will learn more about PHP and Laravel. If you're looking to improve your knowledge on any of these subjects, this book will help you. Be forewarned: there is a ton of really bad humor in this book. Here is an example.

My pappy once told me, two days ago, that all great books have at least three things. He asked if I knew what those three things were. I replied,

1. Words

2. Sentences

3. Paragraphs

Wrong! He slapped me with a trout. He corrected me:

1. Cuss words

2. Death sentences

3. Paraphernalia, sex, drugs, and alcohol

"But that's more than thre...," I questioned him, but I was reprimanded with yet another trout slap. "Okay," I said. I quickly shut my yapper. Reader beware, this book has all those things. Don't let your kids read this unless they are over 30 and living in your basement. In that case, tell them to read this book and go get a job.

⚠ Disclaimer   I don't do drugs. This book might make you think otherwise but honestly, I don't need drugs to act stupid. Yes, really.

Who Is This Book For?

Anyone with a sawbuck can be the proud owner of this book. That's the only requirement. But it will help a lot if you already know at least a little bit about PHP or Laravel. If you work on web apps and you've ever found yourself cussing at your past self from 6 months ago, then you'll probably enjoy this book.

You will not be interested in this book if

1. You are a zombie who eats cats.

2. You don't have $10.

3. You'd rather use assembly language than PHP.

4. You invented the Internet.

5. You can bench press 624lbs, exactly.

6. You hate reading really long lists.

7. You think cows should never be given a typewriter.

8. You think David Hasselhoff is cute.

9. You were born yesterday.

10. You run marathons...

11. … backwards.

12. You've never jumped on a bed.

13. You like to spit on pigs.

14. You didn't see *Watchmen* movie only because of the changes made to the story.

15. You would use php-snow[1] for every project, ever.

16. You think Ents are dumb.

17. In fact, if you hate *Lord of the Rings*, stop now and I'll give you your money back. HATER.

18. You pass gas in elevators and smile wildly at other people at the same time.

19. That last one only counts on elevators in buildings over 50 stories high.

20. You work for the FBI or CIA. You are cool but please don't read my book.

21. You have had unusual thoughts about Smurfette. Shame on you and shame on me.

22. You count sheep to stay awake.

23. You can't read.

24. You still blog about TV series *Full House*.

25. You troll books (don't ask me how).

26. You hold deep conversations with Nick Jr. Face[2].

27. You believe aliens don't exist.

28. You work for the FBI (gonna list this twice just in case you didn't catch it the first time).

29. You walk like a penguin and evilly plot against Batman.

30. You were born the day before yesterday.

31. You didn't watch *The Hunger Games* because you've already read the book.

32. You think Zelda is a dude in a green outfit.

33. You will code in Rails until the day you die (good for you, good for you).

34. You are not a zombie but still eat cats.

35. You like to wear dresses in winter and you name is Pat.

36. You can ignore the previous line about dresses (I have a friend who does this).

37. You can find your entire life story in a Dr. Seuss book.

38. You go to the library, find people, and tell them spoilers to great novels.

39. You don't quite understand peaches.

40. You've never seen *Back to the Future*.

---

[1]https://code.google.com/archive/p/php-snow/
[2]www.youtube.com/watch?v=LaXIL8QMDzU

41.   You are in a *Josie and the Pussycats* cover band.

42.   You think Michael Bay should direct every movie, ever.

43.   You are Michael Bay.

44.   You visited the moon and didn't bring me back a moon rock (jerk).

45.   You can do 100 consecutive push-ups (you are too badass to be reading this book).

46.   You were born tomorrow.

47.   You think Chewbacca is chewing tobacco.

Did you really read this entire list? Awesome! I want to talk about gloves. Design patterns are like gloves. If they fit, wear 'em. On the flipside, don't try to wear gloves that don't fit. Learning when to wear your design gloves is important. It is my hope that with the aid of this book you'll understand when to leave the gloves off or put the gloves on. We are almost ready to get started with Laravel basics but first let's go over the structure of this book.

Layout of the Book

The first chapter provides some Laravel basics to get started coding. The next chapter covers elementary OO concepts. From there on out, you start learning different patterns and applying them in the context of Laravel and PHP.

I created a branch for every pattern in a git repository. You can view the git repository at https://github.com/kdocki/larasign[3]. At the beginning of every chapter will be git command to check out that chapter's relevant code samples. You will need to clone this repository down if you want to follow along with code examples.

```
$> git clone git@github.com:kdocki/larasign.git
```

This book organizes the patterns in a similar fashion as the Gang of Four book. The GoF patterns book came out 20 years ago in 1994, and the patterns are still being seen and talked about even in 2014. To me, that is awesome. As you learn some of these patterns, you will also be using the PHP framework Laravel and hopefully pick up little bits and pieces of the framework along the way. You will see that the Laravel framework lets you write quality code. In this book, I will cover these patterns.

Creational

- Abstract Factory
- Builder
- Factory Method
- Prototype
- Simple Singleton
- Simple Factory

---

[3]https://github.com/kdocki/larasign

Structural

- Adapter
- Bridge
- Composite
- Decorator
- Facade
- Flyweight
- Proxy

Behavioral

- Chain of Responsibility
- Command
- Interpreter
- Iterator
- Mediator
- Memento
- Observer
- State
- Strategy
- Template Method
- Visitor

CHAPTER 1

■ ■ ■

Laravel Basics

If you're going to be doing PHP development, you should download Laravel. Symfony and Laravel are the most popular and best frameworks for PHP in the world. To get Laravel on your machine you can follow the instructions on the quick start page[1]. You will need PHP7 with the OpenSSL, PDO, Mbstring, Tokenizer, and XML PHP. It also requires PHP version 5.6.4 or above enabled. You know how to install those, right? Awesome. But just in case, on Ubuntu, use the following code.

Install PHP and a Few Dependencies

```
> sudo add-apt-repository ppa:ondrej/php

> sudo apt-get update

> sudo apt-get install php7.0 php7.0-curl php7.0-mcrypt
```

Now, to create a new laravel app we simply follow the instructions provided to us on https://laravel.com/docs/5.3/installation#installing-laravel inside the folder named designpatterns. As you build out various applications in the book, consult the git branch for each chapter so you git Jedis can trace along.

The next thing you will do is look at Composer. Laravel is built off of about 20 Composer packages; Composer is the cat's meow (see Figure 1-1 for important information).

---

[1]http://laravel.com/docs/quick

© Kelt Dockins 2017

K. Dockins, *Design Patterns in PHP and Laravel*, DOI 10.1007/978-1-4842-2451-9_1

Figure 1-1. Meow

What Is Composer?

Composer is **the** dependency management tool for PHP. It allows you to list the packages your application depends upon to function correctly. A file in the root of the project named composer.json allows for plenty of configuration options, so let's brush over some of those.

Composer does several neat things:

- Dependency management with packages

- PSR and custom file-based autoloading

- Compiler optimization to help code run faster

- Custom hooks into lifecycle events, such as application installed, updated, or first created.

- Stability checking

With your favorite text editor, open up the composer.json file inside the project root. Note that throughout this book file names will all be relative to the project root. Just to be clear here, when I say **project root**, that means directly inside the designpatterns folder you created, so app/MODELS/User.php is actually the path /home/kelt/book/designpatterns/app/models/User.php on my machine.

Meta Information

In the first part of the Composer manifest, you see basic meta information.

composer.json

```
"name": "laravel/laravel",
"description": "The Laravel Framework.",
"keywords": ["framework", "laravel"],
"license": "MIT",
```

All of this information is used by a web site called Packagist[2], which catalogs packages out there in the wild. As a standard practice, if you create packages to host on Packagist you'll probably want the name the same as the GitHub repository for that package.

Dependency Management

Next you see a require block. Here is where package dependency management comes into play. Currently you are only requiring the Laravel framework, which is made up of many other packages; however, as time goes on you will add additional packages.

composer.json

```
"require": {
    "php": ">=5.6.4",
    "laravel/framework": "5.3.*"
},
```

Seems pretty straightforward, right? One gotcha here though is that you might see a ~4.1 or >=1.0,<1.1 | >=1.2. Visiting https://getcomposer.org/doc/01-basic-usage.md#package-versions explains the different rules for versions, as does reading Table 1-1.

Table 1-1. *Version Rules*

Name	Example	Description
Exact version	1.0.2	You can specify the exact version of a package.
Range	>=1.0	By using comparison operators you can specify ranges of valid versions.
	>=1.0,<2.0	Valid operators are >, >=, <, <=, !=.
	>=1.0,<1.1 | >=1.2	You can define multiple ranges, separated by a comma, which will be treated as a **logical AND.** A pipe symbol | will be treated as a **logical OR.** AND has higher precedence than OR.
Wildcard	1.0.*	You can specify a pattern with a * wildcard. 1.0.* is the equivalent of >=1.0,<1.1.
Tilde Operator	~1.2	Very useful for projects that follow semantic versioning. ~1.2 is equivalent to >=1.2,<2.0.

---

[2]http://packagist.org

Although it isn't shown here, you could add a mapping for development only packages by using `require-dev`. Some good candidates for development only packages are **behat**, **phpspec**, and **clockwork**.

Autoloading

Earlier I mentioned that Composer comes with an autoloader and even optimizes the PHP to run faster. It knows how to do this because of the `autoload` section.

composer.json

```
"autoload": {
        "classmap": [
            "database"
        ],
        "psr-4":{
            "App\\": "app/"
        }
},
```

You can also use PSR autoloading. If you've never heard of PSR, take a moment and go to `http://petermoulding.com/php/psr`. Basically it deals with standardizing the folder structure, namespace, and class names of PHP.

Laravel 5 uses psr-4 autoloading unlike it's predecessor Laravel 4. If you look inside of composer.json you will notice these lines

```
"psr-4": {
  "App" : "app/"
}
```

This allows us to reference a file such as app/Services/FooService.php with the fully qualified namespace `use App\Services\FooService;` inside another php file.

Now your application will look inside the app folder and autoload any files from that directory for you. Pretty nifty, right?

Lifecycle Hooks/Scripts

Below are a list of scripts you execute after running `composer install` or `composer update` or `composer create-project` (respectively).

composer.json

```
"scripts": {
        "post-root-package-install": [
            "php -r \"file_exists('.env') || copy('.env.example', '.env');\""
        ],
        "post-create-project-cmd": [
            "php artisan key:generate"
        ],
        "post-install-cmd": [
            "illuminate\\Foundation\\ComposerScripts::postInstall",
            "php artisan optimze"
        ],
        "post-update-cmd": [
            "illuminate\\Foundation\\ComposerScripts::postUpdate",
            "php artisan optimize"
        ],
},
```

You can tap into certain events of composer if you want to run custom commands here. I use these hooks to automatically run things like migrations any time composer install is executed on the server. When you deploy to production servers, you just follow this simple two-step process:

1. git pull

2. composer install

You don't have to remember to run migrations or clean assets or whatever else because you do that after composer install finishes running.

What is the difference between composer install and composer update?

Running composer update will do two things.

1. It will update all required packages to the latest version matched.

2. It will update composer.lock with exact versions of dependencies.

Running composer install will install the dependencies listed in composer.lock. If the lock file does not exist, this command becomes identical to composer update because it will create the composer.lock file for you after downloading dependencies.

Why do we do this?

Let's say you ran Composer on **machine 1** and later on **machine 2**. You need to ensure that the packages are exactly the same on both machines. If you run composer update, the versions of packages could very well differ machine to machine. This can cause problems. Imagine that a particular package you required as a dependency changes a feature. Suddenly **machine 2** is throwing a big fat **500 Internal Server Error** while **machine 1** is still working fine. You always want to avoid that kind of behavior.

Ideally you want your production, staging, and various local environments to be as similar as possible.

You could fix this problem by removing the vendor folder from `.gitignore` and committing **EVERYTHING**, but there is a better way. The lock file will already have the specific github commit hashes, which should not change, and you can use this to your advantage by following the following basic principle:

 Only run `composer` `update` on your local development box. Never on production.

Stability

Now you've come the end of your `composer.json` file.

composer.json

```
"config": {
        "preferred-install": "dist"
},
```

Composer can fetch your dependencies through source code or a distributed zip file. This config option is telling Composer to use prefer distribution files over source code. You can read more about config options at `https://getcomposer.org/doc/04-schema.md#config`.

The `minimum-stability` flag is used to keep other packages from inherently installing unstable versions of other packages into your application.

- You **require** package A.
- Package A **requires** package B@dev.
- Composer will squawk about it.

The squawking happens because your stability is set to `stable` but a subpackage is dependent on an less stable version. In this case, package A depends on a development version of package B.

How would you fix this? In this scenario, in order to install package A, you need to explicitly add package B@dev to the `require` array. Another way to fix this, for brave developers only, is to change the `minimum-stability` to one of the following: `dev`, `alpha`, `beta`, `RC`, or `stable`.

Running Composer

You can download composer via `http://getcomposer.org/`. Once installed, verify your installation by running

```
> composer -v
```

There are a lot of commands you can run with Composer. One example is instead of editing your `composer.json` with a text editor, you can run the Composer command to require dependencies:

```
> composer require
```

Another good Composer command to use is `validate`. Despite all my JavaScript training, I still manage to leave trailing commas, which is invalid JSON, so it is a good practice to validate your `composer.json` file after changes.

Setting Up Your Environment Variable

Laravel offers easy management of environmental variables for your application. Look in your newly created laravel application for a file named .env. This file will contain something like this:

```
```
APP_ENV=local
APP_KEY=
APP_DEBUG=true
APP_LOG_LEVEL=debug
APP_URL=http://localhost

DB_CONNECTION=mysql
DB_HOST=127.0.0.1
DB_PORT=3306
DB_DATABASE=homestead
DB_USERNAME=homestead
DB_PASSWORD=secret

BROADCAST_DRIVER=log
CACHE_DRIVER=file
SESSION_DRIVER=file
QUEUE_DRIVER=sync

REDIS_HOST=127.0.0.1
REDIS_PASSWORD=null
REDIS_PORT=6379

MAIL_DRIVER=smtp
MAIL_HOST=mailtrap.io
MAIL_PORT=2525
MAIL_USERNAME=null
MAIL_PASSWORD=null
MAIL_ENCRYPTION=null

PUSHER_APP_ID=
PUSHER_KEY=
PUSHER_SECRET=
```
```

This .env file allows you to setup different servers using the same application. You can imagine we might have a staging server with a different .env settings file than our production server.

More information can be found on dot env files here: https://laravel.com/docs/5.3/configuration#environment-configuration.

Feel free to experiment here with different configuration files and environments. Die and dump is very useful for quickly debugging in Laravel. It is not a replacement for good tests or Xdebug, though. Now that you've learned some basics in Laravel, let's continue onto SOLID principles.

CHAPTER 2

■ ■ ■

Let's Grow a SOLID Garden

```
$> git checkout solid_design
```

In 2009, a game called Farmville exploded on Facebook. **My mother was addicted; I might have been too but I'm too proud to admit it.** We aren't going to create another Farmville but let's do something similar.

In this chapter, you are going to skim over the five SOLID principles that Robert C. Martin first introduced in his writing called *Principles of OOD*. You'll create a digital garden in this showcase. There was a farmer who planted a garden. E-I-E-I-O.

```
$garden = new App\EmptyGarden(20, 30); // this is a pretty good size\
20x30' garden
$items = $garden->items();     // no plants here, just handfuls of dirt\
```

Single Responsibility Principle

The first principle of SOLID is the single responsibility principle. It states that a class should have a single responsibility.[1] A good practice to follow is to list the responsibility of the class in the comment doc-blocks. This way you can remind yourself and others the purpose of this class and try to keep the responsibility minimal.

app/EmptyGarden.php

```php
namespace App;

<?php

/**
 * @purpose
 *
 * Provides empty garden space full of dirt which can
 * grow and produce items.
 *
 */
class EmptyGarden
{
        private $width;
        private $height;
```

---

[1]http://en.wikipedia.org/wiki/SOLID_(object-oriented_design)#Overview

© Kelt Dockins 2017
K. Dockins, *Design Patterns in PHP and Laravel*, DOI 10.1007/978-1-4842-2451-9_2

```php
    public function __construct($width, $height)
    {
            $this->width = $width;
            $this->height = $height;
    }

    public function items()
    {
            $numberOfSpots = ceil($this->width * $this->height);
            return array_fill(0, $numberOfSpots, 'handful of dirt');
    }
}
```

You could have instead called the `items()` method `harvest()` but that implies that a garden can harvest itself. Generally a farmer or harvester plucks the sweet nectar from our gardens. Gardens just take up space and collect growing things. Harvesting themselves means adding another responsibility.

ℹ Don't take the single responsibility principle too far. The less change a class experiences, the less all these principles really matter. It would be okay to add `harvest()` to the `EmptyGarden` class if it never really changes.

Remember that using principles has trade-offs. If it is easier to maintain one larger class rather than five decoupled smaller classes, don't fight the tide. Encapsulate what varies and leave the rest alone. Also, leave the witch from Left 4 Dead alone, too.

Open/Closed Principle

```php
$garden = new App\MarijuanaGarden(10, 10);
$garden->items();        // about a  day's worth for Seth Rogan
```

Figure 2-1. You were promised drugs, remember?

Wait a minute. Why did you create a MarijuanaGarden? Was it because of the dog (see Figure 2-1)? Wouldn't it be easier to just pass the string Marijuana to the Garden class? On the surface, it would seem easier; it is certainly less classes to track. Ultimately, though, going down the string path results in writing some conditional logic (if, else, switch) and the Garden class would need to be modified each time you wanted to add a new type of garden.

The O in SOLID stands for the open/closed principle and states that classes should be **open for extension but closed for modification.**[2]

---

[2]http://en.wikipedia.org/wiki/SOLID_(object-oriented_design)#Overview

If every time a new type of garden arises you have to modify this Garden class, then you are violating the open/closed principle. The `items()` method returns different items depending on the type of garden. Notice that the approach below allows you to easily add many gardens without ever modifying the original Garden class:

app/Marijuana

```php
class MarijuanaGarden extends EmptyGarden
{
        public function items()
        {
                return array_fill(0, $this->width * $this->height, 'weed');
        }
}
```

Liskov Substitution Principle

The next SOLID principle is called the Liskov substitution principle, which is tough considering PHP is a duck-typed language. It doesn't have strict variable types. However, PHP does have type-hinting, so let's use that.

Objects in a program should be replaceable with instances of their subtypes without altering the correctness of that program.[3]

What happens if when you create an `EmptyGarden` you pass a string or a class or negative numbers for your width and height?

```php
> new EmptyGarden("foo", -1);
```

That's not good! That causes stuff to break. Is that a risk you want to take? Perhaps you can do a little refactoring here. Instead of making your garden depend on `width` and `height`, let's make it depend on a `PlotArea`. This can be an interface that takes up some area of space.

src/EmptyGarden.php

```php
public function __construct(use App\PlotArea; $plot)
{
        $this->plot = $plot;
}
```

What does a `PlotArea` look like? It's an interface, of course!

app/PlotArea.php

```php
namespace App;

interface PlotArea
{
        public function totalNumberOfPlots();
}
```

A `PlotArea` tells you how many plots you have available to plant in this plot area. A circular garden might have 20 plots and a radius of 10 feet. A rectangle shaped garden might have 40 plots for a 10 by 10 foot area. Notice it is an interface and not a concrete class.

You need to change your `EmptyGarden` and `MarijuanaGarden` classes now.

---

[3]http://en.wikipedia.org/wiki/SOLID_(object-oriented_design)#Overview

app/EmptyGarden.php

```php
public function __construct(PlotArea $plot)
{
        $this->plot = $plot;
}

public function items()
{
        $numberOfPlots = $this->plot->totalNumberOfPlots();
        return array_fill(0, $numberOfPlots, 'handful of dirt');
}
```

But how do you call your EmptyGarden now? PlotArea is not a class, it's an interface. What if you create a RectangleArea class that implements PlotArea?

app/RectangleArea.php

```php
namespace App;

use App\PlotArea;

class RectangleArea implements PlotArea
{
        private $width;

        private $height;

        public function __construct($width, $height)
        {
                $this->width = $width;
                $this->height = $height;
        }

        public function totalNumberOfPlots()
        {
                return ceil($this->width * $this->height / 2);
        }
}
```

Now you can tinker with your classes.

php artisan tinker

```php
$garden = new App\EmptyGarden(new App\RectangleArea(10, 10))
$garden->items();
```

You have 50 handfuls of dirt! So much dirt! Pig-Pen from Charlie Brown would be so proud. Why is he so dirty anyway? Where are his parents? How does he keep from getting wicked staph infections?

Another way to break LSP is by returning different types from the same method. In strongly typed languages like Java, this isn't as big of an issue; in PHP, it can be a problem.

Imagine if you called $garden->items(); what would you expect the return type to be? An array, right? What if MarijuanaGarden instead returned a string? This could get messy quickly! It also breaks the Liskov substitution principle.

Unfortunately, if you are using php 5 then you will be unable to set return type-hints on methods[4]. Good news though, return type-hints are a new feature in php 7! Thus you can use the following syntax (see below):

---

[4]https://wiki.php.net/rfc/returntypehint2

13

```php
public function items() : array { ... }
```

If you are still using php 5 then you can still use doc-blocks and @return annotations. This won't help the compiler any but it can help other developers looking at your code. If you are using php 7 then I definitely recommend using type-hinting. If you aren't careful, it is very easy to break the Listov substitution principle in PHP by returning different types in subclass methods.

Interface Segregation Principle

If something is found to be useful, it must change, right? You want to add more functionality to your gardens. Gardens grow plants. You have seeds planted in the ground and after a bit of work and good luck, those seeds grow and yield fruit.

app/GardenInterface.php

```php
namespace App;
{
        public function grow($advanceNumberOfDays);
}
```

This is fine. However, gardens are also fertilized, watered, weeded, prone to attacks from pests such as bugs and rabbits, and depend on weather factors such as sunshine and rain. That's a lot of responsibility for a single class. Let's see what that might look like if you add some more methods.

app/GardenInterface.php

```php
namespace App;
{
        public function grow($advanceNumberOfDays);
        public function weed($pickOutPercentage);
        public function pestAttack($attackFactor);
        public function water($inGallons);
        public function sunshine($radiationLevel);
        public function fertilize($type, $amount);

        ...
}
```

Holy methods, Batman! Notice as this interface grows larger, so does the responsibility of any concrete class that implements GardenInterface. This means the single responsibility principle is likely being violated as well. When you violate one of the five SOLID principles, chances are that other principles are being violated as well.

The SOLID principles work together in harmony. The main problem here is that you are shoving a lot of functionality into a Garden when ideally you could encapsulate the different behaviors. The more functionality you put into a single class, the more difficult it is to manage that class.

It is often so easy to get caught up in domain modeling and thinking about entities that we forget that object-oriented programming is not just creating objects for "things." Encapsulating behavior is a powerful part of OO design. We might have an object called Cat which is an actual thing (noun). Also, we might also have an object called CatMeows, which is more of an action verb than noun. If you aren't already confused enough, just remember *not every object poops.*

Also, what if you wanted to have the grow() method only? Would you implement all of these other methods just to get that one method? You could make a garden just a collection of subinterfaces.

src/GardenInterface.php

```
interface GardenInterface implements GrowableInterface, WeedableInterface, ...
{
}
```

Having a master interface made up of smaller interfaces is certainly a lot more flexible because it allows you to pick and choose from those small interfaces but it doesn't solve the problem of your garden becoming more and more complex. Ultimately, you will end up adding more classes to address this problem. For now, you can just create empty methods for the EmptyGarden class.

Keeping your interfaces small follows the interface segregation principle: *many client-specific interfaces are better than one general-purpose interface.*[5]

Dependency Inversion Principle

The DIP (dependency inversion principle) states that *one should depend on abstractions instead of concretions.*[6] What does this mean? To answer that question, recall earlier when you defined a PlotArea for your garden; what if instead you had done this:

app/Garden.php

```
public function __construct(RectangleArea $plot)
{
        $this->plot = $plot;
}
```

This would have forced you to use a rectangle area for every garden. If you need gardens to be a variety of shapes, this wouldn't work at all. So to avoid the problem of being inflexible, you use an abstraction (PlotArea interface) in place of a concretion (RectangleArea class). This aspect of dependency inversion is known as dependency injection and is accomplished by injecting in classes that implement a specific interface.

Another sure way to pick up on violations of dependency inversion is when you start seeing new keywords in your code. Imagine if you had just created a new rectangle area inside the items() method.

app/Garden.php

```
public function items()
{
        $numberOfPlots = new RectangleArea; // oh no's!
        return array_fill(0, $numberOfPlots, 'handful of dirt');
}
```

In this example, the EmptyGarden class is a high-level class and depends on a low-level class RectangleArea. See the word new?

At some point in your application you will likely use the word new to create an object. This is fine, but it does mean that the class is coupled with another class and a hard dependency is made. There's nothing wrong with creating objects with a new, but do it in the wrong places and it can lead to brittle, coupled code that is more challenging to test and maintain. I try to keep my new statements in higher-level code and factories (you'll learn more about factories later).

---

[5]http://en.wikipedia.org/wiki/SOLID_(object-oriented_design)#Overview
[6]http://en.wikipedia.org/wiki/SOLID_(object-oriented_design)#Overview

In software engineering, there is a saying: *low coupling, high cohesion*. Coupling is the degree to which one class relies on another class. Cohesion is the degree to which elements inside a class belong together.

Pretend your class was an island; you'd want things to work well inside of it. Good economy, low crime, etc. If your island does rely on other countries, then you want to keep it minimal. Why? Imagine if one of those countries unfriends you on Facebook, causing your economy to tank. Now your people are starving. Not cool. Definitely not cool. So depending on very few outside countries is an example of both low coupling and high cohesion. The best island is the one that works well by itself and doesn't let dependencies overwhelm it. Again, *low coupling, high cohesion*.

To mitigate cohesion and coupling issues, follow the practice that high-level classes should not depend on low-level classes and vice versa. Instead, depend on abstractions such as an interface, abstract class, etc.

How do you know a high-level from a low-level class?

Picture a high-level class as a maestro who is conducting a concert. The low-level classes are the people playing the instruments in the band. The conductor is orchestrating the lower-level classes and the result is *beautiful music*.

However, imagine the maestro depended on a concretion: Bob the tuba player. If Bob is out sick with the flu, the maestro must shut down the big concert. What if instead of depending on Bob, he depends on the abstraction: tuba player. In marches Fred, a different type of tuba player but nonetheless tonight's show is saved! The maestro doesn't have to worry if it is Bob, Fred, or Sally playing the tuba, just so long as they qualify as a tuba player. This is dependency injection at its finest.

One point to note: *dependency inversion is not the same thing as dependency injection*. Another way to do dependency inversion is by using an inversion of control container.

app/Maestro.php

```php
class Maestro
{
        public function conduct($song)
        {
                $tubaPlayer = app()->make('tuba.player');
                $clarinetPlayer = app()->make('clarinet.player');

                foreach([$tubaPlayer, $clarinetPlayer] as $player)
                {
                        $player->play($song);
                }
        }
}
```

Notice that you are not depending on any type of class here. Instead you let app()->make() provide you with the tuba player and clarinet player needed. They could easily be swapped out in the service container.

app/Providers/PlayerServiceProvider.php

If Composer is the backbone of Laravel, then the service container is the brain. You'll learn more about Laravel's service container in later chapters.

Conclusion

Here are some tips summed up by principal.

Single Responsibility Principle

Don't put all your worker eggs in a single basket. A class should have one reason to change.

Open/Closed Principle

Don't change the same class over and over. If you find this happening, abstract out what is changing.

Listov Substitution Principle

Return the same type in an overridden subclass method as a parent class method. The same applies for a method's parameters. Be consistent.

Interface Segregation Principle

Don't create interfaces with many (more than five) methods. This is a sign that you're doing too much in one place.

Dependency Inversion Principle

Rely on interfaces and abstract classes more than concrete classes. This will be more flexible.

Encapsulate What Varies

Only abstract away things that vary in your application. For example, if an `Mailer` class will never change, don't get hung up on writing a lot of abstraction around that: *focus on what will change*.

CHAPTER 3

Abstract Factory

```
$> git checkout abstract_factory
```

Intent

Provide an interface for creating families of related or dependent objects without specifying their concrete classes.[1]

Applications

When you have a family of objects that are somewhat related, you can use a factory to create products. Sometimes you want to create variations of a product. A product could be *any class*. It could be a User, Airplane, or House. When dealing with real estate, commercial is different than residential. In this case, you might create two factories: one for commercial and one for residential. The residential factory could produce products such as a house and land. The commercial factory could products like a store building and lots. The real estate client could still do operations such as sell, buy, and list on the lot, land, house, and store building. You don't have to change your client when you change your factories.

---

[1]*Design Patterns: Elements of Reusable Object-Oriented Software*, p. 99

© Kelt Dockins 2017
K. Dockins, *Design Patterns in PHP and Laravel*, DOI 10.1007/978-1-4842-2451-9_3

Abstract Structure

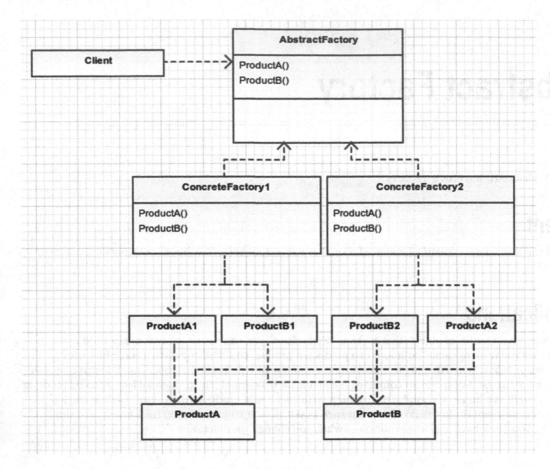

Figure 3-1. *This is an abstract uml document of abstract factory. It's all abstract!*

- **Client:** This class uses the abstract factory. See Figure 3-1. The concrete factory can be passed as an argument to the client's constructor or the client can be smart enough to know which concrete factory to use without dependency injection. For example, a client might decide to use a family based on the operating system running (Windows, Linux, or Mac).

- AbstractFactory: This can be an interface or abstract class that is implemented by the concrete factory. If you use an abstract class, then the default behavior can be built into the base abstract class.

- ConcreteFactory (1 and 2): These classes inherit from the AbstractFactory and generate the products for their concrete type of family. There are only two ConcreteFactories shown in Figure 3-1 but there could be more if needed.

- Product (A and B): These are abstract classes or interfaces that will be implemented by concrete product classes A1, B1, A2, B2, and so on.

- Product (A1/B1 and A2/B2): These classes all belong together in a family. A1 and B1 are in a different family than A2 and B2, though, so they are created by different factories. These are the classes that you care about and get used by the client in some way.

Example

You are creating a simulator that can be run in PG-13 or R rated mode. The name of the game is Garden Ninja. Plants are grown in gardens and merchants sell or consume those plants. You can create all sorts of variations of fruits and vegetables. You can sell produce in a variety of ways. The basic steps for a merchant are

1. Grow a garden.

2. Sell produce.

The goal of the game never changes. What changes is the underlying **family** of products drafted upon the player, which can change in respect to the player's maturity level.

You are going to create two diverse families of garden merchants:

1. Drug dealers

2. Rice farmers

A rice farmer will grow a rice garden. The rice farmer won't grow and sell rice the same way as the drug dealer. The drug dealer is producing illegal marijuana so his actions will likely be surreptitious.

Example Structure

Figure 3-2 shows the example structure.

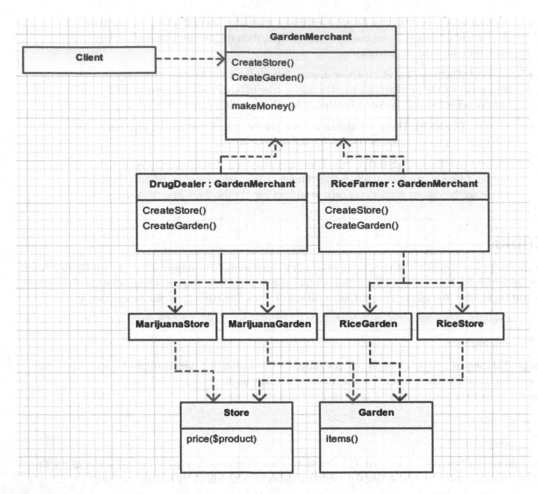

Figure 3-2. *Put it all together and make a family of related objects. Rice farmers and drug dealers are related by a family of products (gardens and stores). Who knew, right?*

Implementation

If you'd like to see this work, download the repository and check out branch `abstract_factory`.

Your simulator will create a new merchant from a random maturity rating and then make money from that merchant. Due to the risk involved, drug dealers in this game make more money than rice farmers. Not that rice isn't risky or anything.

app/simulator.php

```php
require __DIR__ . '/../vendor/autoload.php';

$ratings = array(
    'PG-13' => new GardenNinja\RatedPG13\RiceFarmer,
    'R' => new GardenNinja\RatedR\DrugDealer
);
```

```
$merchant = $ratings[array_rand($ratings)];

$client = new App\Client($merchant);

$client->run();
```

There are a lot of missing pieces here. Let's start by examining the Client class.

```
class Client
{
        public function __construct(Merchant $merchant)
        {
                $this->merchant = $merchant
        }

        public function run()
        {
                print "Your merchant made $" . $this->merchant->makeMoney() . PHP_EOL;

        }
}
```

Next, the Merchant class acts as the abstract factory that is used by the Client class in this example.

app/Merchant.php

```
<?php namespace App;
```

```
abstract class Merchant
{
        abstract public function createStore();
        abstract public function createGarden();
```

You rely on your concrete factories, which implement Merchant to create your two products: stores and gardens. All merchants attempt to make money, so you place that method in this abstract class.

app/Merchant.php

```
public function makeMoney()
{
        $makeMoneyMoneymakeMoneyMoney = 0;
        $store = $this->createStore();
        $items = $this->createGarden()->items();
        foreach ($items as $item) {
                $makeMoneyMoneymakeMoneyMoney += $store->price($item);
        }
        return $makeMoneyMoneymakeMoneyMoney;
}
```

If you understand how the RiceFarmer class works, you should understand how the DrugDealer class works. They are related because they are both in the Merchants abstract family. So let's take a look at the RiceFarmer class.

app/RatedPG13/RiceFarmer.php

```php
<?php namespace App\RatedPG13;

class RiceFarmer extends Merchant
{
        public function createStore()
        {
                return new RiceStore;
        }

        public function createGarden()
        {
                return new RiceGarden;
        }
}
```

Pretty simple, right? RiceStore is just in charge of pricing products and the RiceGarden creates new Rice items for us to sell. However, you could get pretty complex here with pricing and how many items are returned in your garden from various outside factors.

When you run php app/Simulator.php you will see that sometimes your merchant makes $20 and other times $300. This all depends on which random rating your simulator runs at and which concrete merchant type was passed to the client.

Conclusion

You used the abstract factory to create a family of products related to the Merchant. Why did you do all this work? You could have made a few conditional statements and accomplished the same results in this simulation. Why create all these classes? How does this benefit you?

In this example, your classes are super simple (RiceStore and RiceGarden). In a real-world example, these classes could be much more complex. Your modular design using the abstract factory pattern allows for growth as you add additional merchants.

In an earlier chapter, you learned to only encapsulate what changes. In your simulator, you could add more merchant types for other vegetables, soybeans, herbs, and spices. You could even support crazier ideas like candy gardens. In doing so, you aren't forced to edit existing classes, only to add more merchant types to the game.

One drawback to the abstract factory is that any changes to your abstract Merchant class would trickle down into all the concrete classes. This means you must think long and hard about the structure of your application and how families of products are grouped together. Later down the road in your example application it might not make sense to group families of products by maturity ratings.

Another drawback is that you could put a lot of effort into using this design and if things need to change dramatically it could be harder to refactor. In your example scenario, there is undoubtedly an easier and better way to structure this application than using an abstract factory design pattern because this contrived example is rather simple. Can you think of any other drawbacks?

CHAPTER 4

Builder

```
$> git checkout builder
```

Intent

Separate the construction of a complex object from its representation so that the same construction process can create different representations.[1]

Applications

A builder is good for creating complex products. As discussed in the last chapter, a product can be *anything*. All the creational patterns focus on producing products. Some products are just naturally complex, though. So in that case, you can delegate the building process to a director and builder. More about that in just a second. A real-life example of the builder pattern is the construction of a car. An assembly line and engineers follow the builder pattern to produce the finished product: a car. When you want fine-tune control over the many steps to create a product, this is your go-to pattern.

---

[1] *Design Patterns: Elements of Reusable Object-Oriented Software*, p. 110

© Kelt Dockins 2017

K. Dockins, *Design Patterns in PHP and Laravel*, DOI 10.1007/978-1-4842-2451-9_4

Abstract Structure

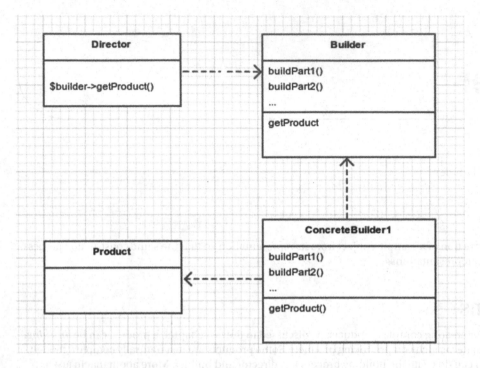

Figure 4-1. *Bob the Builder says, "YES WE CAN!"*

- **Director:** This class contains a set of instructions (an algorithm) that controls the builder's actions. The specific instance of a builder can be passed as a constructor or as a parameter to a public method on the director class. See Figure 4-1. You will use the latter approach in your example.

- **Builder:** This is the abstract base class or interface that has all the steps listed that can be used to construct a product.

- **ConcreteBuilder:** This class inherits from the abstract Builder class and holds the actual methods that create the product. There can be as many different builders as needed. This class will yield a specially created Product.

- **Product:** This is a complex object, generally with lots of nuts and bolts or moving parts, and it is not easily constructed. It is likely made up of many different properties.

Example

Sometimes people make complex things. As the son of a contractor, I am a first-hand witness that building a house is no trivial task. A lot of work goes into the construction process. Luckily, there are blueprints from an architect to guide the entire process. These blueprints are the architect's list of instructions on how to build the house. The same blueprints read by two different carpenters can produce different results, though.

A few years ago, I lived in a three bedroom, two bathroom house in the suburbs. In this scenario, you are going to recreate my house. The Architect will be playing the role of the director and you will have a NoviceCarpenter and ExpertCarpenter building my old house from the same architect's instructions.

Example Structure

Figure 4-2 shows the structure.

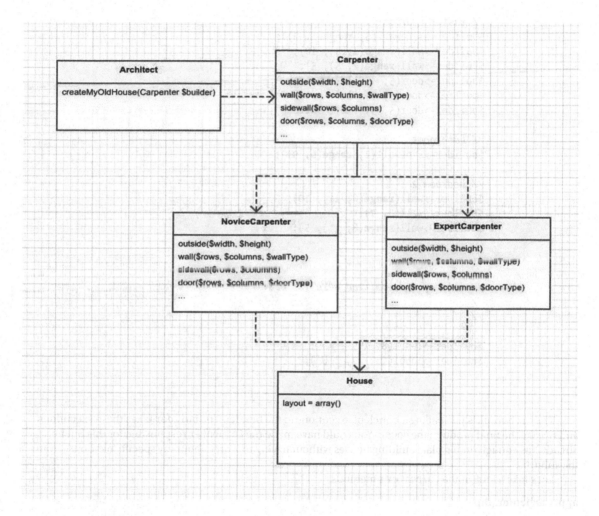

Figure 4-2. *Building a house*

Implementation

In this scenario, the Architect will be the director and direct the different Carpenters (the builders) on how to build the house. The product you really care about is the house, but in order to get a house you must use a carpenter, and to make it easier you also use an architect.

app/Architect.php

```php
namespace App;
{
        public function createMyOldHouse(Carpenter $builder)
        {
                // house foundation
                $builder->outside(25, 13);

                // master bedroom
                $builder->sidewall(5, range(1, 9));
                $builder->wall(range(1, 5), 10);
                $builder->wall(range(2, 5), 5);
                $builder->door(5, 4, 'left bottom');
                $builder->door(1, 5, 'left bottom');
                $builder->door(5, 9, 'left bottom');

                // bathrooms
                $builder->sidewall(2, range(6, 9));

                // bedroom 2
                $builder->wall(range(8, 11), 10);
                $builder->wall(8, 7);
                $builder->wall(range(8, 11), 5);

                //
                //
                // lots of code omitted here for brevity
                //
                //

                $builder->label(8, 21, ' K');
                $builder->label(11, 22, ' U');
        }
}
```

The Architect is just calling a bunch of executions to the builder. The builder takes these executions and tweaks the final product: the House. You could have made the Carpenter responsible for this but he already has enough on his plate building houses without having to worry about my specific old house from the suburbs.

Let's take a look at the Carpenter's methods.

app/Carpenter.php

```php
namespace App;
{
        protected $house;

        public function __construct(House $house = null)
        {
                $this->house = $house ?: new House;
        }
```

```php
        public function getHouse()
        {
                return $this->house;
        }

        public function outside($width, $height)
        {
                $this->house->layout = array_fill(0, $height, array_fill(0, $width, "  "));
                $this->topOutsideWall($width, $height);
                $this->leftOutsideWall($width, $height);
                $this->rightOutsideWall($width, $height);
                $this->bottomOutsideWall($width, $height);
        }
        abstract public function wall($rows, $columns, $wallType = 'left side');
        abstract public function sidewall($rows, $columns);
        abstract public function door($rows, $columns, $doorType = 'left entry');
        abstract public function blank($rows, $columns);
        abstract public function label($rows, $columns, $label);
        abstract public function topOutsideWall($width, $height);
        abstract public function leftOutsideWall($width, $height);
        abstract public function rightOutsideWall($width, $height);
        abstract public function bottomOutsideWall($width, $height);

        protected function items($rows, $columns, $item)
        {
                // put the item where it needs to go inside the house
        }

        protected function assertInBounds($row, $column)
        {
                // make sure the requested row/column is inside of the house
        }
}
```

The Carpenter is taking on the role of the builder. In this application, you have two types of Carpenters, though, who behave differently, namely the Novice and the Expert. These carpenters will produce a different house using the same set of instructions given by the director (your Architect). It would be super easy to add more builders (e.g. DrunkenCarpenter) to your application later if you needed. Let's look at NoviceCarpenter.

app/NoviceCarpenter.php

```php
namespace App;
{
        public function wall($rows, $columns, $wallType = 'left side')
        {
                $this->items($rows, $columns, $this->wallChar($wallType));
        }
```

```php
    public function sidewall($rows, $columns)
    {
        $this->items($rows, $columns, '--');
    }

    public function door($rows, $columns, $doorType = 'left entry')
    {
        $this->items($rows, $columns, $this->doorChar($doorType));
    }

    public function blank($rows, $columns)
    {
        $this->items($rows, $columns, '  ');
    }

    public function label($rows, $columns, $label)
    {
        $this->items($rows, $columns, $label);
    }

    public function topOutsideWall($width, $height)
    {
        $this->items(0, range(0, $width - 1), '--');
    }

    public function leftOutsideWall($width, $height)
    {
        $this->items(range(1, $height - 1), 0, '| ');
    }

    public function rightOutsideWall($width, $height)
    {
        $this->items(range(1, $height - 1), $width - 1, ' |');
    }

    public function bottomOutsideWall($width, $height)
    {
        $this->items($height - 1, range(0, $width - 1), '--');
        $this->items($height - 1, 0, '|-');
    }

    protected function wallChar($wallType)
    {
        // returns the correct wall character for this type
    }

    protected function doorChar($doorType)
    {
        // returns the correct door character for this type
    }
}
```

The NoviceCarpenter implements your abstract methods and uses specific types of material, the | and – characters. The ExpertCarpenter builds things with the sturdier = and) characters because he is more experienced.

Finally, if you run your simulator, you get some nice ASCII art of the layout of my old home.

app/simulator.php

```
require __DIR__ . '/../vendor/autoload.php';


$director = new App\Architect
$builder1 = new App\Architect
$builder2 = new App\Architect

$director->createMyOldHouse($builder1);
$director->createMyOldHouse($builder2);

print '-- Novice Carpenter --' . PHP_EOL;
print $builder1->getHouse();
print PHP_EOL . '-- Expert Carpenter --' . PHP_EOL;
print $builder2->getHouse();
```

```
$ php app/simulator.php
-- Novice Carpenter --
------------------------------     -------------------
|              Ba      |     \                        |
|            |-------- |                              |
|   MB       |         |                              |
|            |  Ba     |                              |
|   -----    | ------  |      LR          --     --  |
| --|        |         |                 | |         |
| --\  --- -- -----|                     | |      K  |
|      \ | |   /|              ----\      ----  |  | |
|        |     |  |          ----\       ----  | |  | |
|   Br   |  Br |  |          |    |       -- | |
|        |     | \ |            |      | | / U| |
|------------------  |-\-------------    | | ----| --
-- Expert Carpenter --
================================ ===================
=              Ba     )     \                   =
=            ) _____)                          =
=   MB       )         )                          =
=            )  Ba     )                          =
=   ____     ) _____   )      LR        ___   __  =
= _)         )                     ) )      )    =
= _____                ) )      )    =
=     (\ ) /)      )                ) )  K  )    =
=         )         )          ___\ ___) )      )    =
=   Br   )   Br    )          ) )   )  ) )   _)  =
=         )         )          \ )   )  ) ) / U)  =
=====================\    ============) ) ====)==
```

Conclusion

Figure 4-3. *Cat skinner blues*

This pattern is useful for cases where you can create different complex objects for the same set of instructions. There are many ways to skin a cat and as tempted as I am to put a cat picture here, I think it would be too much for my Photoshop skills (see Figure 4-3). Think for a moment about how you would separate the algorithm from the actual cat skinning part. You could use the Builder pattern and end up with different sets of instructions (directors) and different cat skinning methods (builders).

A downside of this pattern is that your director is coupled to your abstract builder. If the builder changes, then so must your director.

CHAPTER 5

■ ■ ■

The Factory Method

```
$> git checkout factory_method
```

Intent

Define an interface for creating an object, but let subclasses decide which class to instantiate. The factory method lets a class defer instantiation to subclasses.[1]

Applications

When you are creating variations of some *thing*, you can break those variations into separate *product* classes. However, these classes may be difficult to construct, so you create accompanying factories for each product. Factories can be used to replace or refactor class constructors so that no logic exists inside the *product* class constructor. This pattern differs from the abstract factory because you are not creating families of products. In fact, an abstract factory can be made up of many different factory methods.

---

[1]*Design Patterns: Elements of Reusable Object-Oriented Software*, p. 121

© Kelt Dockins 2017
K. Dockins, *Design Patterns in PHP and Laravel*, DOI 10.1007/978-1-4842-2451-9_5

Abstract Structure

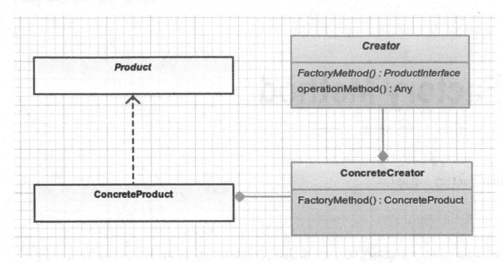

Figure 5-1. *The factory method uses a concrete subclass to create a concrete product.*

- **Creator:** The abstract class that acts as the interface for all concrete creators. This will likely contain shared functionality used by all/most concrete creators. If factories don't differ for each type of product, then this can become a single concrete creator itself and is no longer abstract. See Figure 5-1.

- **ConcreteCreator:** When the creation of a concrete product has different creation logic, then you override the Creator base class with a creator specifically for the ConcreteProduct.

- **Product:** The abstract class or interface that is used by all ConcreteProducts.

- **ConcreteProduct:** This is a variation of Product. It contains logic specific to its variation. This object is created by a ConcreteCreator.

Example

You are going to grow plants. The type of garden yields different types of plants. If your factory is a marijuana garden, then it creates marijuana plants. The product your garden factories manufacture are plants but the concrete plant type is marijuana. A vegetable garden might yield corn, squash, and potatoes as the products. A vegetable garden is another concrete type of your factory interface, Garden. Corn, squash, and potatoes are concrete types of your product interface, Plant. Hopefully that makes sense.

Example Structure

Figure 5-2 shows the structure.

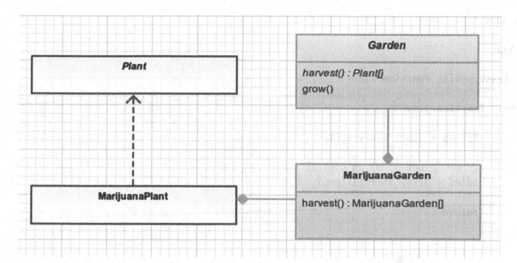

Figure 5-2. *Please don't send the FBI to my house.*

Implementation

Here is your simulator that will grow your garden. Once a garden is grown, you can iterate over the plants returned and consume them. Notice how you can swap out the marijuana garden with a different garden factory and the rest of the simulator can run unaltered. For now, you'll stick to drugs.

app/simulator.php

```
$garden = new App\MarijuanaGarden
$plants = $garden->grow();

foreach ($plants as $plant) {
        $plant->consume();
}
```

In case you're wondering what marijuana garden looks like, I'm not going to show you a picture here. How about a class instead?

app/MarijuanaGarden.php

```
namespace App;
{
        public function harvest()
        {
                return [new MarijuanaPlant, new MarijuanaPlant]
        }
}
```

Notice you are extending the Garden class. This could be an interface but you are going to inherit some basic functionality from the abstract garden class, as you can see below. Plants can die, just like people. It really is sad but it always happens. In your garden, one plant always dies. Please don't ask me why.

app/Garden.php

```php
namespace App;
{
        abstract public function harvest();

        public function grow()
        {
                $items = $this->harvest();

                // one plant died, oh noes!!!
                $died = array_shift($items);

                return $items;
        }
}
```

Next, you should check out what a marijuana plant looks like. Again, no pictures for you here; couldn't get the dang camera to work.

app/MarijuanaPlant.php

```php
namespace App;
{
        public function consume()
        {
                print "you now have a strong hunger for a bag of Bugles" . PHP_EOL;
        }
}
```

Conclusion

The factory method pattern makes it easy to bring in other types of plants later down the road. The different variations and combinations of plants are easy to construct with your factories. The main take-away point is to abstract away difficult construction process of a class.

You might be wondering how the factory method pattern differs from the abstract factory pattern. The abstract factory is used to create families of (sometimes vastly different) products, and the factory method is really concerned with creating a single varying product. Abstract factories often use factory methods.

One drawback to this pattern is that sometimes it may be overkill for what you're trying to do. A more simplified/watered-down version of the factory method is called the simple factory, and I will discuss it in a later chapter. Factories are extremely useful, especially when used in conjunction with domain-driven design. In applications with heavy logic, factories will be your ally.

CHAPTER 6

Prototype

```
$> git checkout prototype
```

Intent

Specify the kinds of objects to create using a prototypical instance, and create new objects by copying this prototype.[1]

Applications

Use the prototype pattern when you want to fork and modify existing objects. A good use for this pattern is when you want to avoid the construction of a class that takes a lot of time or is complicated to create initially. An example of an object with a costly creation is one that uses a web service to fetch data. Once you have the data, though, you no longer need to fetch data from the web service; you just clone the data. There is another pattern called *proxy* which is also a good candidate for the web service example described here. As you will see shortly, you can also use this pattern for cloning complex objects.

Abstract Structure

Figure 6-1 shows the structure.

---

[1]*Design Patterns: Elements of Reusable Object-Oriented Software*, p. 133

© Kelt Dockins 2017
K. Dockins, *Design Patterns in PHP and Laravel*, DOI 10.1007/978-1-4842-2451-9_6

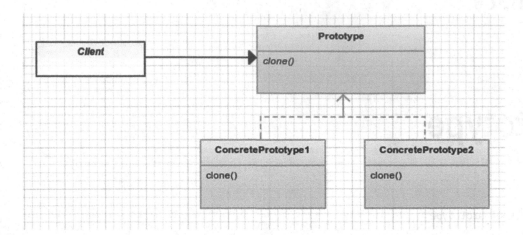

Figure 6-1. *Clone, clone, everywhere a clone*

- Client: Uses the Prototype class. This can be a class or the script itself. In this example, you won't even worry about the client.

- Prototype: This is an abstract class that other classes can extend. It does not have to be abstract, though, if there is only one ConcretePrototype. The clone method is used to make copies of the internal structure of the class so you can create a new object with the same internal structure.

- ConcretePrototype (1/2): These classes extend from the Prototype class and can have extra methods for each variation of prototype. If there are no variations of the prototype, you could potentially merge this in as the Prototype.

Example

The world changed forever on July 5th, 1996 when Dolly the sheep was born as the first mammal to be cloned from an adult somatic cell. The newborn Dolly was given her name because she was cloned using mammary glands, something that the singer Dolly Parton is particularly notorious for. Dolly died from a retrovirus that attacked her repository system. Lung issues are actually common in clones. This is why you are going to keep track of the lungs for every sheep in your simulator.

Example Structure

Notice in Figure 6-2 that you are not creating variations of sheep in this example; therefore ConcretePrototype1 becomes Prototype.

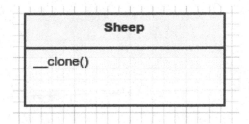

Figure 6-2. *Example prototype structure*

Implementation

You are going to use PHP's native, built-in cloning mechanism to apply the prototype pattern. This isn't a requirement to implementing the prototype pattern since you could create your own clone methods; however, getting to know the native php-clone is much easier and cooler, in my unprofessional opinion.

Pretend you have sheep...

app/Sheep.php

```php
namespace App;
{
        public $name = "Big Momma";
}
```

Now that you've established the presence of sheep, I'm feeling quite ecstatic because I have some really bad sheep jokes to tell you.[2]

- What do you call a sheep covered in chocolate? *A Candy Baa.*

- What do you get if you cross an angry sheep and a moody cow? *An animal that's in a baaaaaaaad mooovooood.*

- How do sheep in Mexico say Merry Christmas? *Fleece Navidad!*

- How many sheep does it take to knit a sweater? *Don't be silly. Sheep can't knit!*

- Where do sheep get their wool cut? *At the baa-baa shop!*

Okay, I hope EWE enjoyed those jokes. Now that I got that out of my system, the next step is to build a simulator that creates and manages sheep for you.

src/simulator

```php
$sheep = new App\Sheep;
$dolly = $sheep;
$dolly->name = "Dolly Parton";
var_dump($sheep, $dolly);
```

Your simulator should spit out the names of $sheep and $dolly for you. You know that Dolly Parton is the name for $dolly; however, what do you think the name is for the starting $sheep in this situation?

---

[2]http://jokes4us.com/animaljokes/sheepjokes.html

simulator output

```
class Sheep#2 (2) {
  public $name =>
  string(5) "Dolly Parton"
 }
class Sheep#2 (2) {
  public $name =>
  string(5) "Dolly Parton"
}
```

Uh oh. It would appear that $sheep->name is no longer Big Momma. If you're used to object-oriented programming and know how memory pointers work, then this is probably no surprise to you. In this example, though, you don't want to worry about the data in your sheep objects being baaaaaaa-ad. You might have noticed that both objects are pointing to Sheep#2. This tells you that both $sheep and $dolly are pointing to the exact same address in memory. In PHP, when one object is set to equal another object, then both objects are referencing the same address space in memory. See Figure 6-3.

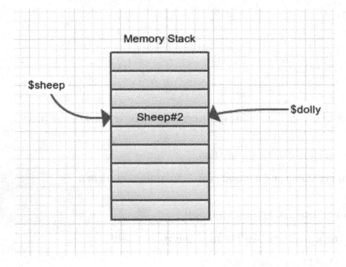

Figure 6-3. *We are the same object, boss!*

If you want them to have different memory addresses, you should clone the sheep instead, which is precisely what you will do.

src/simulator

```
$dolly = clone $sheep;
```

This utilizes another memory slot and copies the $name variable to the new memory address. Now when you update the name of $dolly, it won't affect the $name of $sheep because it is using an entirely different address in memory. See Figure 6-4.

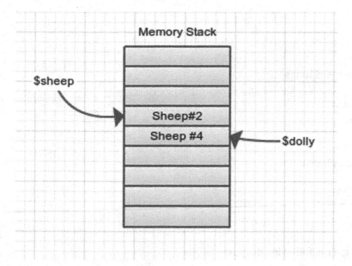

Figure 6-4. *Cloning at its finest*

If you run your simulator again, you can see the output is exactly how you want it to be.

simulator output

```
class Sheep#2 (2) {
  public $name =>
  string(5) "Big Momma"
}
class Sheep#4 (2) {
  public $name =>
  string(5) "Dolly Parton"
}
```

All is well, for the time being; however, you haven't really implemented prototype pattern here yet. The next thing you want to do is modify your sheep class to add in at least one composite.

app/simulator.php

```
$sheep = new App\Sheep(new App\Lungs);

$dolly = clone $sheep;
$dolly->name = "Dolly Parton";
$dolly->applyVirus('JaagsiekteVirus');
var_dump($sheep, $dolly);
```

Before you run your simulator you should give sheep Lungs (a new class) and also add the applyVirus method to the Sheep class. This method will apply damage to the lungs of the sheep. Much like the health meter for a Mortal Kombat character, lungs have a health meter. Health ranges from 0 to 100 percent; when a new sheep is born, the lungs are at 100% health capacity. After applying the JaagsiekteVirus, the lung health goes to 20 percent.

app/Sheep.php

```php
namespace App;
{
        public function __construct(Lungs $lungs)
        {
                $this->name = "Big Momma";
                $this->lungs = $lungs;
        }

        public function appyVirus($virusType)
        {
                $this->lungs->health(20);
        }
}
```

Now when you run your simulator you get the following output:

simulator output

```
class Sheep#2 (2) {
  public $name =>
  string(9) "Big Momma"
  public $lungs =>
  class Lungs#4 (1) {
    protected  $health =>
    int(20)
  }
}
class Sheep#3 (2) {
  public  $name =>
  string(12) "Dolly Parton"
  public  $lungs =>
  class Lungs#4 (1) {
    protected  $health =>
    int(20)
  }
}
```

Uh oh, again. You cloned the sheep, but the clone is a shallow copy of only the primitive internal variables. This means that two different sheep with different names share the same set of lungs in your simulation. This should not happen, so you need to force a deep clone and create different lungs anytime your sheep are cloned. To fix this issue, you use the magical clone method.

app/Sheep.php

```php
public function __clone()
{
        $this->lungs = clone $this->lungs;
}
```

Now anytime a sheep is cloned, so are their lungs. This keeps sheep AND lung objects from sharing memory addresses. The drawback to cloning is that more memory address space is used, so you should be careful not to clone objects unless it is really needed. Running your simulator again shows the correct output.

simulator output

```
class Sheep#2 (2) {
  public $name =>
  string(9) "Big Momma"
  public $lungs =>
  class Lungs#4 (1) {
    protected  $health =>
    int(100)
  }
}
class Sheep#3 (2) {
  public  $name =>
  string(12) "Dolly Parton"
  public  $lungs =>
  class Lungs#5 (1) {
    protected  $health =>
    int(20)
  }
}
```

That about wraps up the prototype pattern. The focus of the pattern is to copy any object references into their out memory address spaces so you can use these objects in isolation of each other. In your example, Sheep is not very complicated but you could add a lot of variables to it to measure the stability and health of the animal in your simulator.

Why not use a simple factory here? This prototype pattern seems like a lot of extra work, no? You could use a simple factory to create the first original sheep. However, what happens if you modified that sheep internally by applying some viruses and yada-yada-yada, you have a different looking sheep. What if you want to start creating clones of that modified sheep? This is where the prototype pattern really excels over a simple factory.

app/simulator.php

```php
$sickSheep1 = clone $sheep;
$sickSheep1->applyVirus();
$sickSheep2 = clone $sickSheep1;

$sickSheep1->applyMedicine('Medicine 1');
$sickSheep2->applyMedicine('Medicine 1');

// compare the health of two sick sheep...
```

Conclusion

You use cloning in this example to easily create duplicate sheep. In this example, the Sheep objects were pretty simple but in a real-life simulator, the Sheep objects could have a lot of variables and data tied to them. Creating new sheep shouldn't be tedious, and you actually care very little about that part. You care more about modifying a sheep and seeing how well it stands up to the viruses. You certainly don't want the construction aspect of new sheep to overwhelm the logic in your simulator.

One drawback to the prototype pattern is that you can easily break the single responsibility principle. A class that already exists has a responsibility, and cloning just adds another responsibility to that class. It is minor, considering that you can clone objects with great ease now.

Another drawback not seen here is that when using the prototype pattern you could end up with different ConcretePrototypes with different methods. This makes it difficult to manage newly cloned objects. For example, imagine if you had two concrete types of sheep called WoolySheep and MilkingSheep. They have different methods: MilkingSheep has a method called gotMilk() and WoolySheep has a method called gotWool(). Now the client has to know which type of sheep you are dealing with. If the client doesn't keep up with this, then the method gotMilk() might be called on a WoolySheep, which would throw an error.

CHAPTER 7

Singleton

```
$> git checkout singleton
```

Intent

Ensure a class only has one instance and provide a global point of access to it.[1]

Applications

Short answer: none. Honestly, I have yet to find any practical applications for the singleton pattern in PHP. The original singleton design pattern was made to ensure that only one instance of a class could ever be created. It was used in the context of printer spoolers where you would only ever want one instance created. Out of the box, PHP is a single-threaded environment and usually has a short lifetime within an apache/nginx thread. Even if you used something like React PHP[2], you can't use blocking operations (sleep, file_get_contents, global) so at no point of your application do you need to worry about restricting global access to a single instance of some class because even in React it would cause deadlocks.

Therefore, you are going to learn a variation that I call simplified singleton. These are singletons that you register in the Laravel service container, or if you're not using Laravel, you could register them in *some* IoC container. However, if you are curious about how to implement the singleton pattern, let's go over that first and then finish the chapter by showing the Laravel service container for singletons.

Abstract Structure

Figure 7-1 shows the structure.

---

[1]*Design Patterns: Elements of Reusable Object-Oriented Software*, p. 144
[2]http://reactphp.org

K. Dockins, *Design Patterns in PHP and Laravel*, DOI 10.1007/978-1-4842-2451-9_7

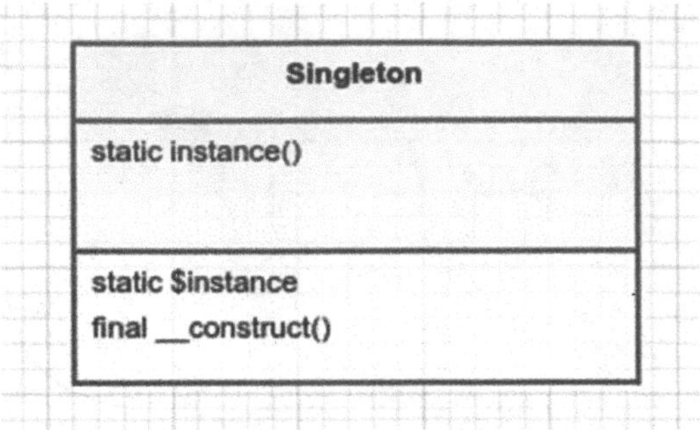

Figure 7-1. *The singleton pattern*

- Singleton: Take note of the protected final restriction placed on the constructor. The constructor can only be invoked from within the class itself. How is it possible to call a method to create yourself if you don't exist yet? It is a chicken-and-egg problem. In this case, though, through the use of static method instance() you can create a new instance of your singleton, which is stored in the protected $instance variable.

Example

In this example, you are going to make a counter that increments each time a request is made. You will try this out both ways: using the singleton pattern and the simple singleton pattern. As an extra bonus, you are going to create the singleton pattern with a PHP feature called a trait[3]. Why? **Because you can.**

Implementation

First things first: you need to create a class that counts requests.

app/RequestCounter.php

```php
namespace App;

class RequestCounter
{
        private $numberOfRequestsMade = 0;

        public function numberOfRequestsMade()
        {
                return $this->numberOfRequestsMade;
        }
        public function makeRequest()
        {
                $this->numberOfRequestsMade++;
        }
}
```

---

[3]http://php.net/manual/en/language.oop5.traits.php

Next, let's talk about traits. What is a trait? If you know this already, you can skip this part. When I first learned about traits, I went gung-ho, using them every which way, left and right. I was trait crazy. It took me a few weeks to realize that I was abusing traits. In PHP, we use traits as a way to mix in functionality. In PHP, we can't extend multiple classes (also known as multiple inheritance). Traits are a way to get around this limitation. Not having multiple inheritance is not a bad thing, though. Regular classical inheritance is difficult enough without adding the ability to inherit from multiple classes. Sometimes we have a small bit of functionality that doesn't belong in any particular class, but we want to add to many different classes; traits are extremely useful for this. Don't go crazy with traits, like I did. Don't get drunk on trait power or you will find yourself a few weeks later with a huge trait hangover headache.

You are going to create a trait called `SingletonPattern` that can be added to any class in order to turn it into a singleton. I said earlier that you'll probably never use Singleton pattern, so you are using this as an exercise to see the cool factor of traits and learn a new pattern.

app/SingletonPattern.php

```php
namespace App;

trait SingletonPattern
{
    static protected $instance;

    final protected function __construct()
    {
        // no one but ourselves can create ourselves
    }

    static public function instance()
    {
        if (! static::$instance) {
            static::$instance = new static;
        }
        return static::$instance;
    }
}
```

Now let's use this trait. You'll create a new class that extends from `RequestCounter` and also uses your `SingletonPattern` trait.

app/RequestCounterSingleton.php

```php
namespace App;

class RequestCounterSingleton extends RequestCounter
{
    use SingletonPattern;
}
```

Wait a minute here. Why did you create a new class like this? The reason is simple and twofold.

1. You want to be able to unit test your RequestCounter class. Testing a singleton is more difficult than a regular ol' PHP class.

2. You are going to use RequestCounter in the Laravel service container later. The service container will take care of the singleton stuff for you and in that case you don't need this SingletonPattern trait.

At this point, you are ready to use your singleton. Again, this is just an example of how you could implement the singleton pattern via traits. There isn't really any practicality of doing so; this is purely an educational attempt to learn about traits.

app/simulator.php

```
App\RequestCounterSingleton::instance()->makeRequest();
App\RequestCounterSingleton::instance()->makeRequest();
App\RequestCounterSingleton::instance()->makeRequest();

// Singleton request hits: 3
print 'Singleton request hits: ' . RequestCounterSingleton::instance\
()->numberOfRequestsMade() . PHP_EOL;
```

Now let's see how you would do a simple singleton using the Laravel service container.

app/simulator.php

```
app()->instance('request.counter', new App\RequestCounter);
app()->make('request.counter')->makeRequest();
app()->make('request.counter')->makeRequest();
app()->make('request.counter')->makeRequest();
app()->make('request.counter')->makeRequest();
app()->make('request.counter')->makeRequest();

// Simple singleton request hits: 5
print 'Simple singleton request hits: ' . app('request.counter')
->numberOfRequestsMade() . PHP_EOL;
```

Each time you call app()->make(), it is reusing the same RequestCounter class. It is doing this only because you used app()->instance(), which pointed Laravel to treat 'request.counter' as a singleton. You can also use the service container to in such a way that it would create a new RequestCounter each time you called app()->make(). If you didn't want 'request.counter' to be a singleton, you would creating a binding instead of an instance, like in the following code.

Binding Example (not a Singleton)

```
app()->bind('request.counter', function ($app) {
  return new RequestCounter;
});
```

At this point you might be wondering why you would use the service container for a singleton instead of just using a global variable. In fact, the service container is a global variable created on line 14 of bootstrap/app.php. So why not use a global variable? Why go through extra work?

bootstrap.app

```
$app = new Illuminate\Foundation\Application(
    realpath(__DIR__.'/../')
);
```

The answer is that by using the service container you have decoupled all clients from the RequestCounter class. You could at any time swap out the RequestCounter with some other class with the same interface and theoretically the rest of your application would keep on keeping on. You would do this by swapping out app()->instance('request.counter', new SomeOtherRequestCounter). This is an incredibly flexible and powerful thing to have in your framework arsenal.

Conclusion

You learned about the singleton pattern and the modified simple singleton pattern. You covered the service container in Laravel and traits. While you likely won't use the singleton pattern, you'll probably at some point find yourself using singletons in the Laravel service container for a variety of reasons, including performance enhancement or sharing data across the system.

CHAPTER 8

Simple Factory Method

```
$> git checkout simple_factory_method
```

The simple factory is not an design pattern you find in the original 90s Gang of Four design patterns book. Yet it is an extremely useful way to create objects—so useful that I made a chapter for it.

Intent

The simple factory method simplifies the process of creating new concrete objects.

Applications

Using a simple factory makes code cleaner and easier to deal with. This pattern can be applied when you want to create an object that has dependencies. This pattern can be used to refactor places in code where products are created. One might say that this is the factory method pattern we discussed earlier. That might be true to an extent. It differs in that we don't create multiple factories for multiple products. We only create a single factory that can produce various products.

Abstract Structure

- Factory: This class creates the Product for you (see Figure 8-1). Sometimes a product takes several lines of code to create because of dependencies; if you are doing this throughout your application, it opens up doors for bugs to sneak into your code. It is also a way to decouple the creation of a Product from all the clients that use it. You could later swap out Product in one single location: the Factory.

- Product: This class can be made up of several dependencies: Subclass1, Subclass2, Subclass3, etc...

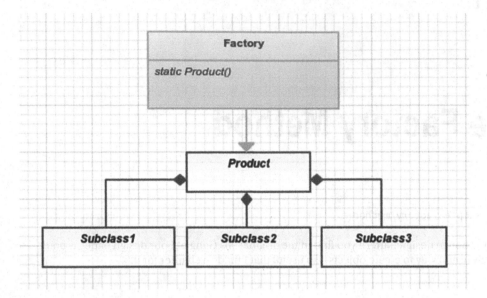

Figure 8-1. *Factory creates a shiny new product for you*

Example Scenario

You are going to refactor the following code to use a simple factory.

Some Contrived Example

```
$bar = new Bar('test', 123);
$baz = new Baz;
$foo = new Foo($bar, $baz);
```

Implementation

If you find yourself doing this same code over and over, then abstract this to a factory make things easier.

Another Contrived Example

```
$foo = Foo::factory();
 // or perhaps using Laravel's service container
$foo = app()->make('foo');
```

Let's look at how you could create this factory method with just simple PHP. Then you will work it into the Laravel service container.

app/Foo.php

```
namespace App;

class Foo
{
        public function __construct(Bar $bar, Baz $baz)
        {
                $this->bar = $bar;
                $this->baz = $baz;
        }
```

```php
static public function factory(Bar $bar = null, Baz $baz = null)
{
        $bar = $bar ?: new Bar('test', 123);
        $baz = $baz ?: new Baz;
        return new Foo($bar, $baz);
    }
}
```

What is happening here? You've basically moved the code to create a new Foo object into this factory method. Now you have the ability to override the dependencies if you choose to do so, but the dependencies are hardwired in by default.

Tinkering Around Inside of Artisan Tinker

```
> Foo::factory()
// object(Foo)(
//   'bar' => object(Bar)(
//     'var1' => 'test',
//     'var2' => 123
//   ),
//   'baz' => object(Baz)(
//
//   )
// )
```

Perhaps you don't like that factory method sitting around in your Foo class. That's a good sign that you should refactor the code somewhere else. Let's make a Factory class for that purpose alone.

app/Factory.php

```php
namespace App;

class Factory
{
        static public function foo(Bar $bar = null, Baz $baz = null)
        {
                $bar = $bar ?: new Bar('test', 123);
                $baz = $baz ?: new Baz;

                return new Foo($bar, $baz);
        }
}
```

Running tinker with App\Factory::foo(); will produce similar results as before.

You might notice that you've been using static methods. Many factory methods are static because it is easier to call them that way. You wouldn't want to have to create a new Factory first and then call the foo method. Why do something in two steps when you can do it in one? Testing isn't an issue here, either. You aren't going to be mocking or unit testing this factory method; you wouldn't gain a whole lot by doing that. The real code you want to test is inside of the classes that the factory is creating.

Conclusion

Simple factory methods clean up classes and put the creation of complex objects with several dependencies in one single place.

It is worth noting that the Laravel service container is smart enough to automatically inject dependencies for you, so take advantage of that when you can.

Service Container Automatic Dependency Resolution

```
class First
{
}

class Second
{
  protected $first;
  public function __construct(First $first)
  {
    $this->first = $first;
  }
}

class Third
{
  protected $second;
  public function __construct(Second $second)
  {
    $this->second = $second;
  }
}

$third = app()->make('Third'); // this works!
```

In this example, the Laravel service container will automatically inject a Second object into the Third object and likewise it will resolve a First object into Second object. This allows you to create clean and **testable** code because all your dependencies are injected into the constructors. When you test the Third class, you can just inject in a mock Second class if you want, which makes things much easier to test because you can focus strictly on Third's public methods (its interface).

At this point, you should know the difference between a simple factory pattern and a factory method pattern. I'll state it again, though, just to be sure: the factory method pattern uses child classes to create different variations of a product class. The simple factory pattern is a simple helper function that replaces the new keyword and cleans up the creation of more complex objects with several dependencies.

CHAPTER 9

■ ■ ■

Adapter

```
$> git checkout adapter
```

Intent

Convert the interface of a class into another interface that the clients expect. Adapter lets classes work together that couldn't otherwise because of incompatible interfaces.[1]

Applications

Sometimes you want to use **existing** code but the interface does not match what you need. For example, you want to utilize vendor/outside code without rewriting all of your **existing** code. It is analogous to fitting a square peg in round hole. A square peg **can** fit inside any round hole, provided the peg is small enough. You should take care to adapt what is needed because the more methods you add to your adapter interface, the larger your square peg becomes inside your round hole.

You might have noticed I highlighted **existing** in the last paragraph. That is because I want to stress the main purpose/intent of the adapter pattern: working with **existing** code. Imagine how impossible it would be to change all of Europe's electrical outlets from 220V to the United States' 110V standard. Sure, if you were wiring a house from scratch, you might wire it with 110V but we aren't starting from scratch. There are millions of apartments, hotels, and homes in Europe, way too many to *refactor*. This is where the adapter shines. Using an adapter lets us keep both existing (and proven) systems in place. We don't change the systems; we only have to worry about the adapter, which is far easier, especially when the two systems are somewhat compatible with each other.

You already know the adapter pattern because you use adapters in real life. Your smartphone plugs into a USB adapter that is plugged into a 110V wall socket. Your computer monitor plugs into a HDMI-to-DVI adapter or Thunderbolt for Mac users. Power adapters convert your car's cigarette lighter into something you can plug your phone into for charging.

To reiterate, you probably won't use the adapter pattern when starting fresh code. It's real benefit comes from adapting **existing** code already set in stone. Okay, talk about beating a deaf horse (Figure 9-1). I'll shut up about when to use the adapter pattern now.

---

[1] *Design Patterns: Elements of Reusable Object-Oriented Software*, p. 157

© Kelt Dockins 2017

K. Dockins, *Design Patterns in PHP and Laravel*, DOI 10.1007/978-1-4842-2451-9_9

Figure 9-1. *Mr. Ed would be proud to call you his son... HORSE PRIDE!*

Abstract Structure

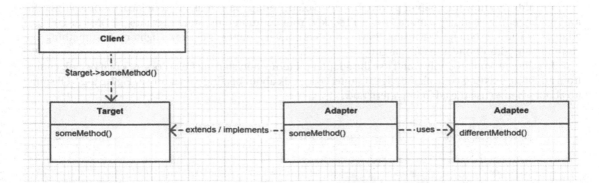

Figure 9-2. *Adapter pattern*

- Client: These are the classes that expect a Target class (Figure 9-2). Since you are dealing with an existing system here, Client might actually be more than just one class.

- Target: This is the interface that the client expects to see. Ideally this is an abstract class or an interface. However, if it is a regular class, then the Adapter can still extend this class and overwrite all the public methods.

- Adapter: This class will extend or implement the Target. It's methods, which match those of Target, are usually wrappers around the Adaptee methods. For example, in Figure 9-2, Adapter::someMethod() calls Adaptee::differentMethod.

- Adaptee: This is the class you are trying to wrap with an Adapter. This class is usually vendor, package, or legacy code that you want to bring into your existing application. It could also be code that you wrote but you are scared to touch because it is old and has no unit tests but has proven to work because it is being used in applications. Whatever the case, the goal is to take this Adaptee code and

Example Scenario

You have existing system that mails letters to an address. This system has been proven to be useful, and now the bigwigs upstairs want to integrate it into your company customer relationship management (CRM) database, which houses many, many client addresses. Your job is to add the feature of mailing to customers from the company CRM database.

Example Structure

Figure 9-3 shows the structure.

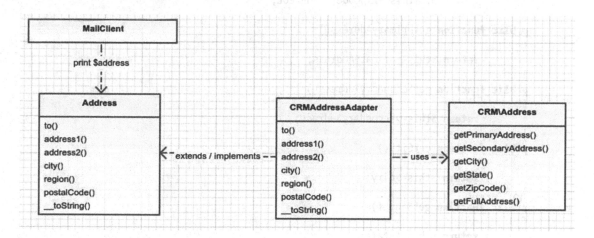

Figure 9-3. *Mail system using the adapter pattern*

Implementation

You could run in, guns ablazing, and attempt to refactor your MailClient or even create a new MailClient, but MailClient is just a small part of the puzzle here and let's assume (although the example doesn't show it) that many things depend on MailClient to work, so creating a new one would take a while to build. Also, you don't want to touch the CRM code, which in this example should be viewed very much like *vendor* code you'd get from a package.

Let's look at the CRM code, which has been provided for you by another team.

app/CRM/Address.php

```php
<?php namespace CRM;
class Address
{
        private $primaryAddress, $secondaryAddress, $city, $state, $zipCode;
        public function __construct($primaryAddress, $secondaryAddress, $ci\ ty, $state,
        $zipCode)
        {
                $this->primaryAddress = $primaryAddress;
                $this->secondaryAddress = $secondaryAddress;
                $this->city = $city;
                $this->state = $state;
                $this->zipCode = $zipCode;
        }
        public function getFullAddress()
        {
                return $this->primaryAddress . PHP_EOL
                        . ($this->secondaryAddress ? $this->secondaryAddress . PHP_'')
                        . $this->city . ', ' . $this->state . ' '
                        . $this->zipCode . PHP_EOL;
        }
        public function getPrimaryAddress()
        {
                return $this->primaryAddress;
        }
        public function getSecondaryAddress()
        {
                return $this->secondaryAddress;
        }
        public function getCity()
        {
                return $this->city;
        }
        public function getState()
        {
                return $this->state;
        }
        public function getZipCode()
        {
                return $this->zipCode;
        }
```

```
        public function setPrimaryAddress($primaryAddress)
        {
                $this->primaryAddress = $primaryAddress;
        }
        public function setSecondaryAddress($secondaryAddress)
        {
                $this->secondaryAddress = $secondaryAddress;
        }
        public function setCity($city)
        {
                $this->city = $city;
        }
        public function setState($state)
        {
                $this->state = $state;
        }
        public function setZipCode($zipCode)
        {
                $this->zipCode = $zipCode;
        }
}
```

This is a pretty straightforward class. I've made it simple but in reality you might have some strange code that is crammed into one giant class with super large methods named doStuff and no comments. You might even have multiple classes you need to adapt. We will cover that later in the Facade chapter but for now let's just stick with the one, simple Address you have here. Next, let's look at your Address class and compare it to CRMAddress.

app/Address.php

namespace App;

interface Address
```
{
        public function to();
        public function address1();
        public function address2();
        public function city();
        public function region();
        public function postalCode();
        public function __toString();
}
```

So the first thing you probably noticed is that you don't even have an Address class; it is an interface. The public methods (the interface) certainly do not match the methods inside CRM\Address. I could show you another class which actually implements; however, that is irrelevant because you are only going to use this interface. Likewise, your adapter will be implementing the Address interface.

app/CRMAddressAdapter.php

namespace App;

class CRMAddressAdapter implements Address
```
{
        protected $to, $Address;
        public function __construct($name, App\CRM\Address)
```

59

```php
    {
            $this->address = $address;
            $this->to = $name;
    }
    public function to()
    {
            return $this->to;
    }
    public function address1()
    {
            return $this->address->getPrimaryAddress();
    }
    public function address2()
    {
            return $this->address->getSecondaryAddress();
    }
    public function city()
    {
            return $this->address->getCity();
    }
    public function region()
    {
            return $this->address->getState();
    }
    public function postalCode()
    {
            return $this->address->getZipCode();
    }
    public function __toString()
    {
            return $this->to . PHP_EOL . $this->address->getFullAddress();
    }
}
```

Here is the simulator code that brings all these pieces of the puzzle together. This is not the Client class you saw in the above UML pattern; the Client here is actually MailClient. The simulator is just running all the different pieces of code. Take notice how the MailClient relies on an Address.

app/simulator.php

```php
$crmAddress = with(new App\CRM\AddressLookup)->findByTelephone('555 867-\
5309');
$address = new App\CRMAddressAdapter('Jenny Call', $crmAddress);
$mailClient = new App\MailClient;
$mailClient->sendLetter($address, 'Hello there, this is the body of \
the letter');
```

I won't cover MailClient here, but basically it sends a message to an Address. I don't show the MailClient class because it really doesn't have anything to do with the adapter pattern. You can see in this simulator you adapted your CRMAddress into Address and passed it to the MailClient. If you had been writing MailClient from scratch in this example, it would have made more sense to skip the adapter pattern and just write the MailClient to depend on CRMAddress instead. Hopefully you now understand how the adapter pattern is used.

Conclusion

The adapter pattern is also known as a wrapper pattern because it wraps an existing interface inside of the interface the client expects. You might find uses for the adapter pattern when you don't have existing code, but most likely this pattern will be used in the case of existing code.

One drawback is that two classes it may be really hard to adapt to so many methods. This can leave your adapter partially broken, and if a client is expecting to use all the methods exposed by the Target interface, then this can lead to problems when the client calls a method that is completely incompatible with the adaptee. Even though target and adaptee have incompatible interfaces, the two are likely related. In fact, why else would you be trying to adapt the adaptee and target for the client if they had nothing in common whatsoever?

Figure 9-4. *Adapter pattern*

Using the adapter pattern, It is possible to make an ambulance *look like* a garbage truck by wrapping an `Ambulance` class inside of a garbage truck adapter class (Figure 9-4). Whether or not that is useful or the best approach depends on the situation. Ambulances are used to deliver people to the hospital in emergencies. Garbage trucks are used to deliver trash to wastelands. They have completely different purposes and goals. However, adapters don't have to be perfect; they only need to implement all public method calls on the target interface the client expects. So if in this case the only method for your Garbage truck class is `pickupTrash`, then although an ambulance would make a terrible garbage truck, there is nothing stopping you from dumping trash inside of this medical vehicle and driving it off to the landfills.

It might prove difficult to adapt two unrelated classes with different purposes but it isn't impossible. Be cautious of creating adapters when a simple refactor would work or when you can create new classes that are more related to solving your problem. For example, in your scenario example, if `MailClient` and `Address` were only used in one or two places in your entire application, it would have been easier to rewrite a new `MailClient` to use `CRMAddress` and throw away `Address`. Long story short, write adapters to keep from doing huge refactors.

Some people confuse the adapter pattern with the strategy pattern. I haven't covered the strategy pattern yet, but the general idea is that both patterns use composition. In fact, a lot of patterns use composition because it is flexible and easier to work with when a change, like a new feature request, occurs later. I covered composition in the early chapters of this book and it's almost always better to use composition instead of inheritance. The strategy pattern is about using composition for switching algorithms while the adapter pattern uses composition to morph/adapt existing interfaces. Also commonly confused with the adapter pattern is the bridge pattern. I will cover the bridge pattern in the next chapter. The two patterns look similar but have different intents. Some patterns look very similar to each other code-wise but the intent is different. I will cover the differences at the end of the next chapter.

CHAPTER 10

Bridge

```
$> git checkout bridge
```

Intent

Decouple an abstraction from its implementation so that the two can vary independently.[1]

Applications

What does it mean to *decouple an abstraction from its implementation*? To show an example of this, let's imagine that you want to send a message. A message is an abstraction. However, there are many different ways you can send a message. You can e-mail it; send it as a letter in the mail; speak it out loud from the rooftops; post it to Facebook, Twitter, or some other web site; put it in a bottle and drop it in the ocean; or fly a banner behind an airplane. Heck, there is even a web site for submitting text messages into outer space[2]. These are all possible implementations of the Message abstraction.

Abstract Structure

- Abstraction is an interface or class that uses methodA from the Implementer. See Figure 10-1.

- RefinedAbstraction is an actual implementation of methodB. Sometimes when using different implementers you need to slightly change your abstraction. You will see this later in the case of MySQL and PostgreSQL connections.

- Implementer is an interface for real implementers *A* and *B*.

- ImplementerA/B satisfy the *Implementer* interface. They both do methodA but in slightly different ways. This method(s) is used under the hood of the *Abstraction* layer.

---

[1]*Design Patterns: Elements of Reusable Object-Oriented Software*, p. 171
[2]www.talk2ets.com

© Kelt Dockins 2017
K. Dockins, *Design Patterns in PHP and Laravel*, DOI 10.1007/978-1-4842-2451-9_10

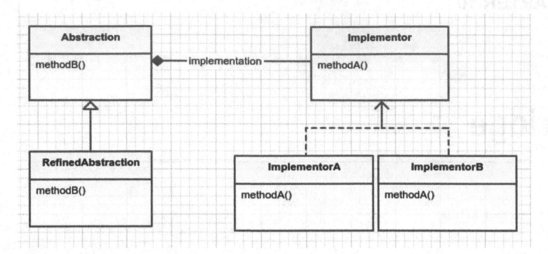

Figure 10-1. *Bridge pattern*

Example

In this example, you are going to take a look behind the curtain at Laravel's schema builder and demonstrate its usage of the bridge pattern. Laravel's schema builder allows you to create new tables and columns in your database, and later roll them back. I will cover this more in the command pattern chapter but for now let's ask this question: how do you build a table in MySQL? What about PostgreSQL? What about Microsoft SQL or SQLite? These are all databases that you'd like to support but if you think about it, you have the following parts:

1.   *Abstraction*: Build a table

2.   *Implementation*: Grammars used to build table in **MySQL, SQLite, PostgreSQL**, etc.

You could create a builder for MySQL, SQLite, and PostgreSQL, but you are likely to write a lot of duplicated code this way. Builders can focus on how to create a table schema, drop a table, or check for table existence. Decoupling grammars that change from database to database allows you to get fine-grained database SQL statements and yet reuse the builder class across the board. As a plus, you will also cover the message example mentioned above.

Example Structure

Figure 10-2 shows the structure.

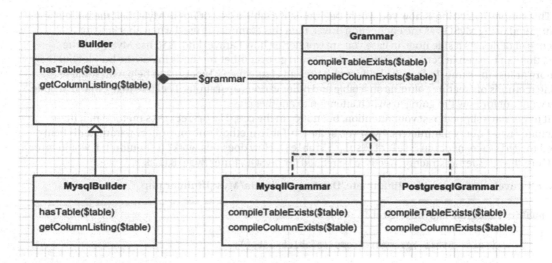

Figure 10-2. *Concrete example*

Implementation

These are rather large classes in Laravel so you are only going to focus on a small subset of code from each class so you can see the builder pattern in action. Let's look at the hasTable method. This method tells you whether or not $table already exists in your database. The builder abstraction relies on the grammar in order to compile the SQL that determines if a table exists or not.

vendor/laravel/framework/src/Illuminate/Database/Schema/Builder.php

```
49    public function hasTable($table)
50    {
51          $sql = $this->grammar->compileTableExists();
52
53          $table = $this->connection->getTablePrefix().$table;
54
55          return count($this->connection->select($sql, [$table])) > 0;
56    }
```

The method hasTable first compiles the database-specific SQL text that determines if a table exists, next it finds the table name with optional global configured prefix, and finally it returns the results of a select run on the SQL code. Let's take a look at compileTableExists on your grammar. You'll use the MySQL version but each database will have their own implementation of this method.

vendor/laravel/framework/src/Illuminate/Database/Schema/Grammars/MySqlGrammar.php

```
33    public function compileTableExists()
34    {
35          return 'select * from information_schema.tables where table_schema \
36    = ? and table_name = ?';
37    }
```

This simple SQL string is how you would determine if a table exists or not in MySQL. If the builder is configured using MySQL as the connection driver, then this grammar is used when checking for the existence of tables. As a side note, in case you are wondering how Laravel knows to use MySQL as the driver, this can be seen in `config/database.php`. I could go over other methods inside the builder but they are more or less the same. In fact, the Builder also uses an class called `Blueprint` to help with some of the routine methods of creating columns on a table and other various operations. Feel free to dig into that code if you want but for now I'm going to switch attention to another class.

It might have slipped past your attention, but notice in the `compileTableExists` method that there are actually two ? query parameters. However, in the `hasTable` method only one query parameter is being passed to `$this->connection->select($sql, [$table])`. How does this work? It shouldn't; it would error out. Thus, the Builder abstraction needs to be refined for MySQL. Enter `MysqlBuilder`.

vendor/laravel/framework/src/Illuminate/Database/Schema/MysqlBuilder.php

```
13   public function hasTable($table)
14   {
15           $sql = $this->grammar->compileTableExists();
16
17           $database = $this->connection->getDatabaseName();
18
19           $table = $this->connection->getTablePrefix().$table;
20
21           return count($this->connection->select($sql, [$database, $table])) > 0;
22   }
```

Apparently to check for table existence in MySQL you need the database name and the table name; therefore the `hasTable` method in `Builder` needs to be refined somewhat to handle this subtle difference. In fact, `MysqlBuilder` only overrides two of the methods in Builder; it leaves the other methods untouched.

Second Example (Sending Messages)

Message in a bottle[3] is not just a Police song, it's also a valid, yet inefficient, way to send messages. Earlier I talked about separating the message abstraction from its implementations. So let's design a system to send messages. Notice the following list of class names. Look at the abstract UML at the start of this chapter and see if you can place them in the correct spot.

- Carrier

- Email

- OceanBottle

- Messenger

- PlainMessenger

Now look at the following classes. How might you use the bridge pattern? What class is the abstraction and which is the implementer? Where is the bridge?

- Carrier (Implementer)

- Email (ImplementerA)

---

[3]`www.youtube.com/watch?v=MbXWrmQW-OE`

- OceanBottle (ImplementerB)

- Messenger (Abstraction)

- PlainMessenger (RefinedAbstraction)

You are trying to abstract the messenger with various carriers. Since Carrier is the implementer, it will hold the logic on how to send a specific type of message.

app/Carriers/Carrier.php

namespace App\Carriers;

interface Carrier
{
        public function sendMessage($message);
}

Email and OceanBottle are both specific implementations of Carrier. Let's take a look at them both. Notice that they just spit out the message. In a real-world example, the email carrier would connect to MailChimp or some service to send your message. The OceanBottle carrier would trigger some machine to print your message out on paper and drop the folded paper into some bottle and throw it into the Pacific Ocean.

app/Carriers/Email.php

namespace App\Carriers;

class Email implements Carrier
{
        public function sendMessage($message)
        {
                echo 'EMAIL: '. $message . PHP_EOL;
        }
}

app/Carriers/OceanBottle.php

namespace App\Carriers;

class OceanBottle implements Carrier
{
        public function sendMessage($message)
        {
                echo 'OCEAN BOTTLE: ' . $message . PHP_EOL;
        }
}

Now that you know how messages are sent, let's take a look at the Messenger class. What is this abstraction for? Remember, the goal of the bridge pattern is to break apart abstraction and implementation. The idea of sending a message is different than the details of actually getting your message sent. If you think about it, the steps you take to send an e-mail are very similar to the steps you take to send a text message or mail a letter.

1.   Put the message onto the medium.

2.   Provide a carrier for the medium.

This isn't to say that the medium and carrier will not change, as they certainly will. An e-mail uses a digital medium and the Internet as a carrier. Letters use paper as a medium and a mail carrier. When speaking your message, your medium is the air and your carrier is a microphone or perhaps a radio broadcast. **Regardless,** the steps remain the same and thus when you abstract away the Messenger class, it handles the two-step process using the carrier and medium for actual details. In this example, you combine the medium and the carrier for simplicity.

app/Messengers/Messenger.php

```php
namespace App\Messengers;

class Messenger
{
        protected $carrier;

        public function __construct(use App\Carriers\Carrier; $carrier)
        {
                $this->carrier = $carrier;
        }

        public function send($message)
        {
                $message = $this->correctMisspellings($message);
                $this->carrier->sendMessage($message);
        }

        // pretend like you are correcting mispellings
        protected function correctMispellings($message)
        {
                return str_replace('Helo', 'Hello', $message);
        }
}
```

Notice that the messenger will attempt to correct your misspellings. Correcting misspellings is **not** the job of the carrier, but you can see how **if** you had **not** separated out the messenger from carrier that this could have been mangled together. What **if** you don't want to worry about spell-checking, though? Much like MysqlBuilder was a refined version of Builder earlier, you will refine your Messenger abstraction and create a PlainMessenger.

```php
{title="src/Messengers/PlainMessenger.php", lang=php}

class PlainMessenger extends Messenger { public function send($message) { return $this->Carrier->sendMessage($message); } } ~~~~~~~~
```

You might want to use the PlainMessenger when you are dealing with a text message type. People like to text emoticons and short words, so spell-checking is less important and could actually be confusing to the user who is sending the text message. In the simulator let's see how to use a different messenger when dealing with the text message carrier.

app/Messengers/PlainMessenger.php

```php
$message = "Helo world!";

$emailMessenger = new App\Messengers\Messenger(new App\Carriers\Email;
$snailMessenger = new Messengers\Messenger(new App\Carriers\SnailMail('PO Box 123,
Somewhere, NY, 12345'));
$textMessenger = new App\Messengers\PlainMessenger(new App\Carriers\TextMessage
('123.456.7890'));
```

```
$emailMessenger->send($message);
$snailMessenger->send($message);
$textMessenger->send($message);
```

Conclusion

You used the bridge pattern to decouple the schema builder from the underlying databases in place. As a simple example, you also used the bridge pattern to build the backbone of a messaging application.

So when should you use this pattern? You might have noticed there is some overhead in splitting an abstraction and implementation into two different classes. In simple cases, using the bridge pattern might be overkill and might add mega confusion bombs to an otherwise simple problem. However, if you are planning for an extensible and flexible ecosystem (e.g. framework) and the bridge pattern seems like a good fit, it probably is. In the above example, you can add new messengers and carriers with ease. It is quite flexible, and each class is very focused. On the other hand, you could have constructed a large `Emailer` class that sends out messages and does spell-checking all in one.

Because you are not separating abstraction and implementations, the cohesive and larger `Emailer` class might be easier to understand for the new blood on the team. Provided you never have to implement a different message carrier, this is nothing wrong which this approach. At a certain point, avoiding a permanent binding between the abstraction and implementations can give you a lot of flexibility.

Your `Messenger` abstraction uses composition to call methods from the `Carrier` implementers. Although you haven't learned the strategy pattern yet, it has a similar structure and uses composition as well. In fact, many of the patterns you learn use composition (because it is badass) and on the surface the patterns can appear akin. Remember, **it's all about intent.** The intent of the bridge is to keep abstractions and implementations very loosely coupled. The intent of the adapter pattern is to act as a man in the middle between two incompatible classes. The intent of the strategy pattern is to encapsulate algorithms. Thus, if you ever find yourself pondering the differences between two patterns, write down their intents and you're likely to answer your own inquiry.

CHAPTER 11

■ ■ ■

Composite

```
$> git checkout composite
```

Intent

Compose objects into tree structures to represent part-whole hierarchies. Composite lets clients treat individual objects and compositions of objects uniformly.[1]

Applications

A lot of things in life have a hierarchical structure: family trees, relationships, organizations, language, nature, military, government, addresses, workplace, games, file structure, and much more. Sometimes things are easier to think about in hierarchies. Imagine trying to try explain your family tree using only first names. Hierarchies allow us to take a complex system and break it down into related parts. We can then introspect the entire tree or just parts of the tree to our advantage.

Hierarchies are naturally thought of as trees. This is because trees start at the bottom and branch off and end up at some particular leaf. The leaf's parent is the branch, and its parent is perhaps another branch. Finally, things end up at the base of the tree. **However**, I don't want you to think that just because we order things in a hierarchy means we have a composite pattern. Note in the intent there is a second sentence: *Composite lets clients treat individual objects and compositions of objects uniformly*. This means that we can call $cat->methodName() and $cats->methodName() and we don't have to worry about the fact that $cat is a single leaf object and $cats is a branch full of leaves of many objects.

Abstract Structure

- Component: This can be an interface or an abstract class that any leaf or composite extends (Figure 11-1). Use an abstract class if there are methods all child classes can benefit from; otherwise, a simple interface will suffice.

- Leaf: A leaf is the primitive Component object. It has no children.

- Composite: A composite is a collection of Components as children. In simple cases, you can store children as an array inside the Composite class. Like the Leaf, it is a Component and thus must implement method.

---

[1]*Design Patterns: Elements of Reusable Object-Oriented Software*, p. 183

© Kelt Dockins 2017
K. Dockins, *Design Patterns in PHP and Laravel*, DOI 10.1007/978-1-4842-2451-9_11

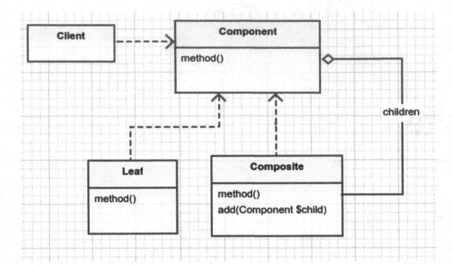

Figure 11-1. *The composite pattern*

Example

If you've built a few web sites, then you've probably dealt with drop-down menus. If you're unlucky, you have one of those clients who wants MEGA menus with a hierarchy of menus with many links. What if you could treat menus all the same, regardless of how many levels there are? You're just printing them off, right? So what if you could just say the following?

Print That Menu Off

```
$megaMenu->print();
// or
$simpleMenu->print();
// or
$someLink->print();
```

Example Structure

Figure 11-2 shows the structure.

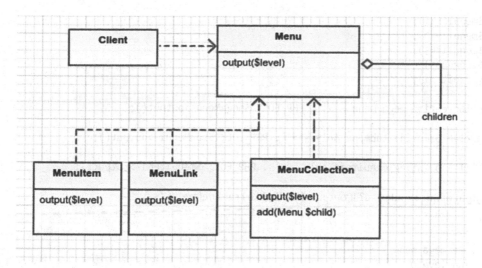

Figure 11-2. Composite pattern for menus

Implementation

What you are building is a way to dynamically output menus. First, though, I want to warn you that putting HTML inside PHP classes is hard to maintain and there is a better way: use a partial Laravel view. However, since this example is purely for illustration of the composite pattern, I went ahead and crammed some ugly HTML inside these classes. At any rate, the goal of this example is to build some menus so that you can easily output them like so:

app/simulator.php

```php
$menulink1 = new App\MenuLink('google', 'http://google.com');
$menulink2 = new App\MenuLink('facebook', 'http://facebook.com');
$menulink3 = new App\MenuLink('kelt', 'http://keltdockins.com');
$menuitem1 = new App\MenuItem('some text');

$megaMenu = new App\MenuCollection;
$subMenu1 = new App\MenuCollection;
$subMenu2 = new App\MenuCollection;
$subMenu3 = new App\MenuCollection;

$megaMenu->add($subMenu1);
$megaMenu->add($subMenu2);
```

```
$subMenu1->add($menulink1);
$subMenu1->add($menulink2);
$subMenu2->add($menulink3);
$subMenu2->add($subMenu3);
$subMenu3->add($menuitem1);

print '<!-- printing entire mega menu -->' . PHP_EOL; $megaMenu->output();

print PHP_EOL . '<!-- printing submenu only -->' . PHP_EOL; $subMenu1->output();

print PHP_EOL . '<!-- printing menuitem1 only -->' . PHP_EOL; $menuitem1->output();
```

What is the output of this simulation? It outputs HTML, like I said before.

Simulator Output

```
<!-- printing entire mega menu -->
<div class="sub-menu level0">
    <div class="sub-menu level1">
        <a title="google" href="http://google.com">google</a>
        <a title="facebook" href="http://facebook.com">facebook</a>
    </div>
    <div class="sub-menu level1">
        <a title="kelt" href="http://keltdockins.com">kelt</a>
        <div class="sub-menu level2">
            some text
        </div>
    </div>
</div>

<!-- printing submenu only -->
<div class="sub-menu level0">
    <a title="google" href="http://google.com">google</a>
    <a title="facebook" href="http://facebook.com">facebook</a>
</div>

<!-- printing menuitem1 only -->
some text
```

Pretty nifty, right? It makes building menus a breeze. You could also add different types of menus, such as a `MenuButton` or `MenuLinkWithImage`. I'm getting ahead of myself, though. You haven't even seen the classes in the above simulation yet. It starts with `Menu`.

app/Menu.php

namespace App;

interface Menu
{
        public function output($level = 0);
}

The rest of the classes extend `Menu` and must implement the output method. Next, let's examine the leaf called `MenuLink`.

app/MenuLink.php

```php
namespace App;

class MenuLink implements Menu
{
        public function __construct($name, $url)
        {
                $this->name = $name;
                $this->url = $url;
        }
        public function output($level = 0)
        {
                print str_repeat(' ', $level * 4);
                print "<a title=\"{$this->name}\" href=\"{$this->url}\">{$this->name}</a>"
                . PHP_EOL;
        }
}
```

As you can probably tell, this class just handles printing out an anchor HTML tag with the URL and name. Pretty simple, right? However, what if you don't have a URL for this MenuLink? You could put in an if statement here, but that means you are adding logic to a method. Is there another way to handle this so you don't have to add an if statement to your output method? How about another leaf? Call it MenuItem.

app/MenuItem.php (typo)

```php
namespace App;

class MenuItem implements Menu
{
        public function __construct($name)
        {
                $this->name = $name;
        }

        public function output($level = 0)
        {
                print str_repeat(' ', $level * 4);
                print "{$this->name}" . PHP_EOL;
        }
}
```

Don't be so quick to create if statements. Remember: the more conditions you have in a method, the harder the method's internals are to understand. Of course, adding a few if/else's here and there won't cause your head to spin backwards but I treat conditionals like frenemies. You have to use conditions but the first chance they get they will stab you in the back, so surround yourself with as few conditions as possible. *Unless you like being stabbed in the back*, in which case, if it up! Anyhow, you solved the problem above by using a different leaf class. Now let's take a look at your composite, lurking in the shadows, masking itself as just another leaf in your hierarchy.

app/MenuCollection.php

```php
namespace App;

class MenuCollection implements Menu
{
        protected $children = [];
```

```php
    public function add(Menu $menu)
    {
        $this->children[] = $menu;
    }
    public function output($level = 0)
    {
        print str_repeat(' ', $level * 4);
        print "<div class=\"sub-menu level{$level}\">". PHP_EOL;

        foreach ($this->children as $child){
            $child->output($level + 1);
        }

        print str_repeat(' ', $level * 4);
        print "</div>" . PHP_EOL;
    }
}
```

This collection handles the output method slightly differently. It calls its immediate children and when those children are also MenuCollections then their children are called. Notice that you can add any type of class that implements Menu to your MenuCollection. Ultimately, this means you can nest links, items, and collections inside a collection.

Before I conclude this chapter, consider this: what if you want to traverse backwards (up) the tree? So if you start a submenu and you want to know its parent, and its parent's parent, etc., right now it's a one way street down, starting from the top level mega menu. You could keep references to each child's parent in a similar way you keep track of its children. It's entirely up to the business needs of your application. If you decide to store parent references, be sure to decide if you want objects to have only one parent or if multiple parents are allowed. When you venture into this territory, you may be dealing with some other pattern besides composite, which is completely fine, so venture on, brave soul!

Conclusion

In this chapter, you used the composite pattern to output a hierarchy of menus. I want to reiterate that simply creating a hierarchy of classes does not mean it is the composite pattern. The composite pattern is seen when individual objects and a collection of objects are treated in the same way. Composite allows you to instruct a single cat to meow() and likewise to instruct a collection of cats to meow(). It lets you output a collection of menus in the same way as a single menu link. Honestly, if you don't have a leaf and you're working with a single composite class, you can call it the composite pattern too. I won't snitch you out to the pattern police, I promise.

CHAPTER 12

■ ■ ■

Decorator

```
$> git checkout decorator
```

Intent

Attach additional responsibilities to an object dynamically. Decorators provide a flexible alternative to subclassing for extending functionality.[1]

Applications

Decorators extend functionality. How are decorators different than mere inheritance? Classical inheritance extends functionality of classes before runtime. Decorators extend functionality of real-time objects during runtime. The decorator *wraps* an real object, giving us the ability to change object behavior at runtime. It may seem weird to talk about *runtime* and PHP, since PHP is an interrupted language and not your traditional compiled language (like C++, Java) but the principle still holds. You are changing behavior dynamically with decorators as the code execution is carried out.

As an example of changing behavior, pretend you have a Duck class and it can quack(). The Duck swims in a radioactive pond and gains superpowers. You can wrap the Duck with a SuperPower decorator, which will now enable him to superQuack(), knocking down bad guys and turkeys that dare to defy duck superiority.

Abstract Structure

- Component: An abstract class or interface that acts as the parent class for ConcreteComponent. If there is only one variation of the component, it may not need to be abstract. See Figure 12-1.

- ConcreteComponent: You may have multiple concrete variations of the Component. This acts as the child class and will be the actual object being wrapped by the Decorator.

- Decorator: This abstract class acts as a base class for all the concrete decorators. This class will most likely share the same public interface as the Component and uses a constructor that takes a Component to wrap. The Decorator public method that is called will typically just proxy the same public method for the Component.

---

[1] *Design Patterns: Elements of Reusable Object-Oriented Software*, p. 196

© Kelt Dockins 2017
K. Dockins, *Design Patterns in PHP and Laravel*, DOI 10.1007/978-1-4842-2451-9_12

77

- ConcreteDecoratorA/ConcreteDecoratorB: These concrete decorators can override methods from the base Decorator class and make use of the wrapped ConcreteComponent object that has been injected via the constructor. In addition to overwriting existing methods, other supplementary methods can be added.

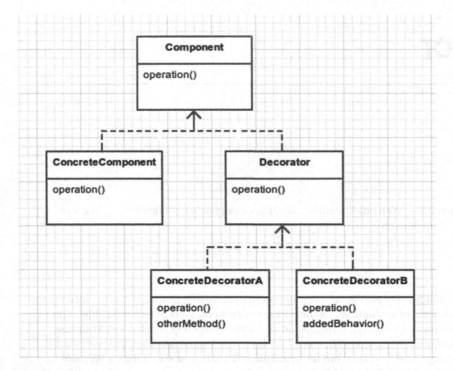

Figure 12-1. Who knew decorating was so much fun?

Example

You are building a game where you have monsters. Each monster has a set strength (STR), intelligence (INT), and speed (SPE). You will wrap decorators around monsters to modify their ability scores at runtime. While there may be a better way to handle lots of monsters (like the flyweight pattern), you aren't worried about memory usage here; you want to focus strictly on adding responsibilities at runtime. During a fight, a monster can morph and adapt to the fight, gaining (and losing) abilities. You don't want to build different Monster classes for all these possibilities; instead, you use the decorator.

I will finish the chapter by talking about presenters, which I will call a slight variation of the decorator pattern.

Example Structure

Figure 12-2 shows the structure.

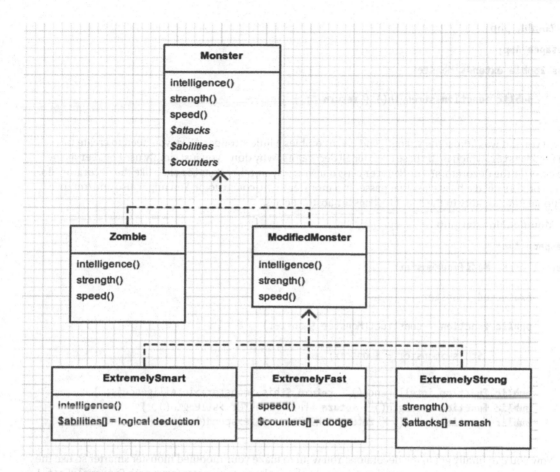

Figure 12-2. Monster Mania@!#$#!

Implementation

Monsters have intelligence, strength, and speed scores. You build a monster class to hold those values.

app/Monster.php

```php
namespace App;

abstract class Monster
{
        public function intelligence() { return 1; }
        public function strength() { return 1; }
        public function speed() { return 1; }
}
```

You need a real monster. I know there is no such thing as monsters or Santa Claus or a monster Santa Claus[2], but monsters exist in video games. Let's pick the dumbest monster of all: the zombie. Classic zombies are not all that scary. You could just walk away from a zombie and it would never catch you. Pop culture movies and games like World War Z and Left 4 Dead have turned these otherwise laughable, slow, dim-witted monsters into fast, strong, horrifying titans[3]. I see no reason why we shouldn't jump on the zombie bandwagon, too!

---

[2]http://en.wikipedia.org/wiki/Santa's_Slay

app/Zombie.php

```php
namesapce App;

class Zombie extends Monster
{
        public function strength() { return 3; }
}
```

All you did was adjust the strength and make zombies a little stronger. Next, you need to create the ModifiedMonster, which is the base class for all decorators. Why don't you just simply use Monster as the base class for the decorators? The Monster class doesn't wrap another Monster class like the decorators do. The decorators need a base class that passes in a monster to the constructor. You might also add/remove additional functionality in the ModifiedMonster abstract class.

app/ModifiedMonster.php

```php
namespace App;

abstract class ModifiedMonster
{
        protected $monster;

        public function __construct(Monster $monster)
        {
                $this->monster = $monster;
        }
        public function intelligence() { return $this->monster->intelligence(); }
        public function strength() { return $this->monster->strength(); }
        public function speed() { return $this->monster->speed(); }
}
```

Now you can finally get to the decorators! You want to make your modified monster smarter so use the ExtremelySmart decorator for exactly that. You could also make your monster faster with ExtremelyFast. I am only showing the ExtremelySmart class because it explains the structure of a decorator. Feel free to look at the other decorator in the source code.

app/ExtremelySmart.php

```php
namespace App;

class ExtremelySmart extends ModifiedMonster
{
        public function intelligence()
        {
                return parent::intelligence() * 2;
        }
        public function castSpell($spell)
        {
                return "casts the {$spell} spell";
        }
}
```

---

[3]http://en.wikipedia.org/wiki/Attack_on_Titan

Lastly, you need a client to run all these decorations. First, you print off the zombie stats.

app/simulator.php

```
5    print 'Running Zombie Thing' . PHP_EOL;
6
7    $monster = new App\Zombie;
8
9    print 'This zombie stats are'
10        . ' STR ' . $monster->strength()
11        . ' INT ' . $monster->intelligence()
12        . ' SPE ' . $monster->speed() . PHP_EOL;
```

Next, you want to add some speed to the zombie. So you modify him at runtime to be decorated with
ExtremelyFast.

app/simulator.php

```
18   $monster = new App\ExtremelyFast($monster);
19
20   print 'Decorated zombie stats are'
21        . ' STR ' . $monster->strength()
22        . ' INT ' . $monster->intelligence()
23        . ' SPE ' . $monster->speed()
24        . ' and it can now ' . $monster->jumpAttack() . PHP_EOL;
```

Now you can add even more speed and intelligence to the Zombie if you want to. He is a super zombie
now, and I'm now scared. I am going to go turn on the lights; it's too dark in here.

app/simulator.php

```
30   $monster = new App\ExtremelyFast($monster);
31   $monster = new App\ExtremelyFast($monster);
32   $monster = new App\ExtremelySmart($monster);
33
34   print 'Decorated zombie stats are'
35        . ' STR ' . $monster->strength()
36        . ' INT ' . $monster->intelligence()
37        . ' SPE ' . $monster->speed()
38        . ' and ' . $monster->castSpell('fireball') . PHP_EOL;
```

Now you know how the decorator pattern works. It attaches additional responsibilities. Note, however,
that if you were to call a jump attack on your monster, it would throw an error.

app/simulator.php

```
41   $monster->jumpAttack(); // no such method - errors
```

The error is caused because the ExtremelyFast decorator provides the jumpAttack but the last
decoration on line 32 was ExtremelySmart, which means that this method is no longer available to you. This
is a downside to the decorator pattern. If a decoration provides some new responsibility that is unknown to
the base ModifiedMonster class, then you only get the latest decoration's methods. Happily, a variation of
the decorator pattern called presenters can deal with this issue.

Presenters

Presenters utilize magic methods[4] in PHP, such as __call()[5] and __get()[6], to get around the disappearing responsibilities issue you discovered in your modified monster decorators. So when do you use presenters? Use them if any of the following are true:

1. **You are adding code to your models strictly for view logic**: Keep your models clean as possible. Models are used *everywhere* in your application. Keep as much logic out as possible to avoid creating demons *everywhere*.

2. **You are adding logic to your Laravel views**: If you find yourself doing lots of conditional statements, consider abstracting this away into a presenter method.

In this example, you will use a presenter called robclancy/presenter[7]. I've taken the liberty of adding it to the composer.json so make sure you run composer update and then you can run the web server with php artisan serve.

Once that is finished take a look http://localhost:8000[8] and http://localhost:8000/presenter[9]. Here are your routes.

routes/web.php

```php
Route::get('/', function () {
        $user = new App\UserPresenter(new User);

        $user->favoriteColor = rand(0, 1) ? 'blue' : null;

        return view('hello', compact('user'));
});
```

Note that I modified the home route for this example. You randomly set a favorite color on this user. You also "decorate" the $user object with a UserPresenter. You will take a look at that class in a moment. First, let's take a look at the hello view. The goal of the presenter is to turn this first bit of code into the second bit of code.

BEFORE

resources/views/hello.blade.php

```php
23   @if ($user->favoriteColor)
24     <span style="background-color: {{ $user->favoriteColor }}">Hello
25   there!</span>
26   @else
27     <span>Hello there!</span>
28   @endif
```

---

[4]http://php.net/manual/en/language.oop5.magic.php
[5]http://php.net/manual/en/language.oop5.overloading.php#object.call
[6]http://php.net/manual/en/language.oop5.overloading.php#object.get
[7]https://github.com/robclancy/presenter
[8]http://localhost:8000
[9]http://localhost:8000/presenter

AFTER

resources/views/hello.blade.php

```
17    <span {{ $user->favoriteColorStyle }}>Hello there!</span>
```

You can see how the second code snippet is just easier on the eyes and doesn't require you to think as much. Believe it or not, it is actually possible to rid your views of most logic. Logicless views are something you should strive for because they make working on your code much easier. Reading thousands of lines of HTML with if/else/else and if/foreach statements thrown in is a real chore. If you never add conditions, then you'll never find yourself debugging logic in your views because it'll be in your PHP presenter class. Speaking of which, let's look at the UserPresenter class.

app/UserPresenter.php

```
namespace App;

class UserPresenter extends Presenter
{
        public function presentFavoriteColorStyle()
        {
                return $this->favoriteColor
                        ? "style=\"background-color: {$this->favoriteColor};\""
                        : '';
        }
}
```

Like I said when we began, presenters are magical, and implementations vary slightly from package to package. There are some other packages out there but I chose robclancy/presenter randomly. You could make your own, but I don't feel like making my own for this chapter. You can, if you'd like, and share it with me. This particular flavor of presenter wants you to prefix present to the Camel cased function name, and that will create a dynamic attribute on your class. You could have just made a function too, but it seems neat to treat favoriteColorStyle as another attribute instead of some function. Perhaps I'm just being lazy, though? Regardless, that covers the variation of a decorator pattern called presenter.

Conclusion

The decorator pattern provides a flexible way to add responsibilities to objects; responsibilities can be attached and detached at runtime. This also means you don't have to code the *perfect class*. If you don't get it right the first time, no sweat. You have the luxury of adding new responsibilities at a later time when the price is right.

A drawback of using decorators is that if you use type hinting, then you have to remember that a Decorator does not implement its Component. It wraps it. Thus, if you using type hinting such as someMethod(Component $obj), this will throw an error because technically a Decorator is not a type of Component. Another drawback to the decorator pattern is that it can become more and more difficult to debug or troubleshoot if you have a lot of decorations going on. Don't let this prevent you from using presenters or decorators, though, especially if you need to extend the responsibilities of classes without subclassing or modifying base classes.

CHAPTER 13

Facade

```
$> git checkout facade
```

Intent

Provide a unified interface to a set of interfaces in a subsystem. Facade defines a higher-level interface that makes the subsystem easier to use.[1]

Applications

Life is hard. Sometimes stuff is just complex. Perhaps the code you are writing is for a really tough problem. Sure, you usually try to break things down to its simplest forms (models) but your modeling doesn't always turn out correct. Sometimes code is complex when it doesn't need to be. When you first write something, you don't always get it right on the first try. How many times have you looked at your older code and wanted to refactor it? You learn new things. You could chance a refactor; however, in some cases that could be very costly (time and money). An alternative to refactoring is to create another layer on top of existing code to make the interfaces easier to understand and work with. In a way, this pattern can be thought of as the **second chance pattern.**

The facade pattern isn't all about covering up bad code, though. It can be used to create a simple public interface that encompasses a wide range of classes working together in some way. Perhaps you're dealing with a large subsystem with hundreds of public methods but you only need ten of them. You want the facade to correctly construct the various classes in the subsystem and provide those ten interfaces to you such that you can use them with ease. Using this pattern lets you think about your code in layers. A facade will wrap a layer of lower-level code so that you don't have to deal with intricate details of that subsystem when you want to utilize the system.

Laravel Facades

 fa-cade (fah-saud)   The front of a building. A way of behaving or appearing that gives other people a false idea of your true feelings or situation.

---

[1]*Design Patterns: Elements of Reusable Object-Oriented Software*, p. 208

© Kelt Dockins 2017
K. Dockins, *Design Patterns in PHP and Laravel*, DOI 10.1007/978-1-4842-2451-9_13

Laravel has something called facades[2], not to be confused with the facade pattern. Laravel uses facades as a way to wrap a class or binding in the service container and then call it *statically*. Thus, if you had a class called AwesomeImpl with a non-static method called someMethod, you could create a facade called Awesome for AwesomeImpl and then call Awesome::someMethod() statically. That's really it, though; it is just about providing a static interface to classes. You don't want static methods in AwesomeImpl because static methods are difficult to test in PHPUnit.

If you follow Laravel drama, then you probably know that every few months someone on reddit[3] complains about facades in Laravel, claiming that they aren't true **facades**. Everyone loves good drama.

> Who cares if they are different? The definition of a facade is a way of behaving that gives people a false idea of a situation. Laravel facades do give the appearance of being classes that have static methods. - *Dramatic Design Feline*

While we are on the subject of the Laravel facade debate, it was mentioned that perhaps Laravel should change the name of facades to proxies. You will learn about the proxy pattern soon. The Gang of Four originally intended proxies for addressing performance, protection, and concurrency. What is the intention of a Laravel facade?

Earlier when I said that Laravel facades where simply used to turn methods into static ones, *I kinda lied.* Sorry. I actually left out one important detail. The true intent of a Laravel facade is to keep the client from having to know how to construct a class. Calling your methods statically is just a by-product. The real reason you call these methods statically is because it is easier to do so. So in the above example, the client never constructs a new AwesomeImpl; the client uses the Laravel façade, which handles construction for them. Calling the methods statically just happens to be sexier to some people than calling them non-statically. Using a Laravel facade allows you to bypass the details of constructing a class. Name the pattern that does that! (I'd say the simple factory pattern.)

At the beginning of the book, I promised some drama, so there you have it! Drama aside, the main takeaway here is that you should be aware that the term *facade* in Laravel carries a different meaning than the facade pattern.

Abstract Structure

Figure 13-1 shows the structure.

- Facade is a single class, typically. It reaches into a complex subsystem and constructs different classes and calls methods. In this abstract example, method() is creating ClassA1, ClassB1, and ClassC1, and calls methods from each. These classes are in the same subsystem so they likely work together somehow. The creator of the facade knows how they work together and created a single method for you to invoke called method(). Thank you, Ghostwriter![4]

- Subsystem contains many classes that all belong together logically. These classes may be in the same Domain. The classes may be somewhat coupled. They may not have anything to do with each other but belong under the same namespace because the developer felt like doing it that way. Understanding the subsystem is crucial to creating the Facade abstraction layer in order to simplify things for everyone else.

---

[2]https://laravel.com/docs/5.3/facades
[3]www.reddit.com/r/PHP/comments/1zpmOy/laravel_lets_talk_about_facades
[4]www.youtube.com/watch?v=HZJSccRDKZc

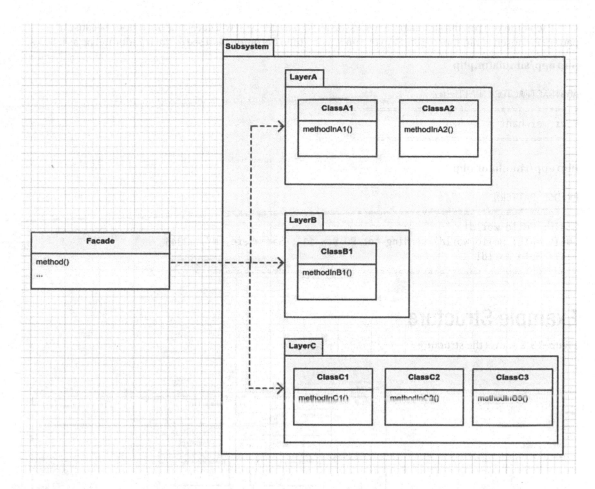

Figure 13-1. *The facade pattern*

Example

I don't have a subsystem of classes for you to use. We need some existing code where we don't quite like the interface. In order to contrive an example, I could go pull some code from WordPress or some other mind-bottling vendor. Alas, though! We only have a hundred-ish years on this blue planet. I do hope you won't be too disappointed if I skip the WordPress idea. We have better things to do with our time.

Therefore, in this example, you are going to take all existing pattern simulations and combine them into one single class. You do this so you can have one place to run all patterns from. You will call this place the PatternExecutor. You are creating a new layer that allows you to trigger the simulation of any pattern you've covered so far. As an extra bonus, there's the random() method whose responsibility is to execute one of the pattern simulations at random. The results should look like the following code:

app/simulator.php

```php
$patternFacade = new App\PatternExectutor;
$patternFacade->random();
```

Each time you run the simulator that uses the pattern façade, you will get a random output because a pattern is chosen at random to run. Say you run it twice, then the output you see might (randomly) be as follows:

php app/simulator.php

```
ABSTRACTFACTORY PATTERN
=======================================
Your merchant made $20
=======================================
```

php app/simulator.php

```
BRIDGE PATTERN
===================================================================
EMAIL: Hello world!
SNAIL MAIL: Hello world! sending to: PO Box 123, Somewhere, NY, 12345
TEXT: Helo world!
===================================================================
```

Example Structure

Figure 13-2 shows the structure.

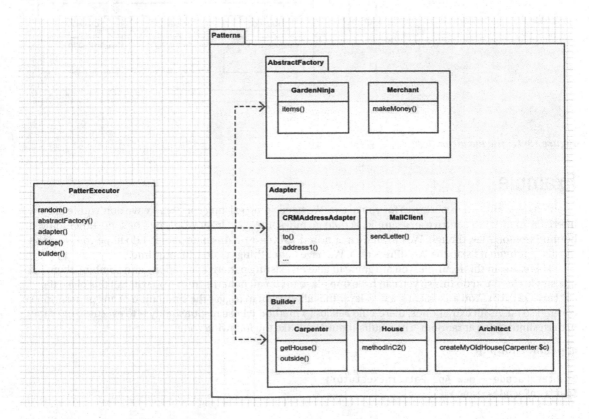

Figure 13-2. *The concrete example*

Implementation

Currently each pattern simulation is within its own branch. This means you need to check out each git branch and copy code over into the /app directory. I only point this out to be clear, and you won't do this in real life with your facade pattern because your code won't be scattered across different git branches in your repository. Now that all the code from the various branches has been copied, imagine that this code is your subsystem. Figure 13-3 is the screenshot of the directory. As you can see, for someone who doesn't know the reason behind this code, the file names don't give much insight.

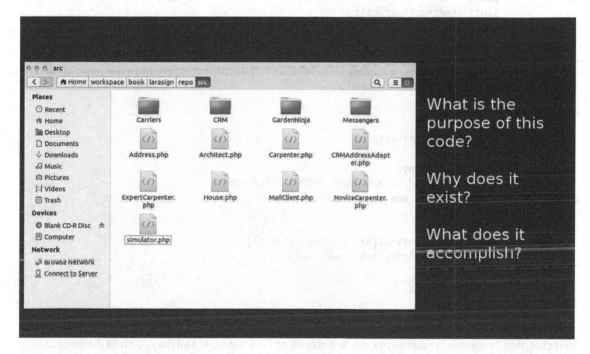

Figure 13-3. What is the purpose of the code in this directory?

Can you tell me the purpose of this subsystem by looking at the file names in the directories? The structure and file names can be confusing. There is a lot going on here, and it isn't clear just by looking at these file names how all this code is supposed to work together. So you are going to create for the newbie developers a facade called `PickerExecutor` that unifies the subsystem of code.

The person who creates code often knows the reason behind the code. They know why a method called `doSomething` exists. They created it. Of course, there is always the element of time and memory loss, so these reasons become less clear. This is why creating a facade may help alleviate any confusion about an entire subsystem's reason for existing.

The facade pattern unifies all this code with a single purpose. What is that purpose? I happen to know that all these classes have the purpose of illustrating GoF patterns but that is because I am the engineer that created the classes throughout the book. Facades are simplifications of complex subsystems, and the complex subsystem here has a purpose of broadcasting different GoF patterns. Thus, your facade will give new users an interface that hopefully has a clear purpose and/or is easier to use. You don't want people to have to dig through all the classes of the subsystem just to utilize the purpose of the subsystem.

app/PatternExecutor.php

```
5    public function random($params = [])
6    {
7            $methods = ['abstractFactory', 'adapter', 'bridge', 'builder'];
8            $method = $methods[array_rand($methods)];
9
10           print PHP_EOL . strtoupper("$method pattern") . PHP_EOL;
11           print "======================================" . PHP_EOL;
12           $this->$method($params);
13           print "======================================" . PHP_EOL;
14   }
```

This random method is picking a random method name and invoking it. So choose a few methods to look at, any of which could be chosen at random.

app/PatternExecutor.php

```
16   public function abstractFactory()
17   {
18           $ratings = array(
19                   'PG-13' => new App\RatedPG13\RiceFarmer,
20                   'R' => new App\RatedR\DrugDealer
21           );
22
23           $merchant = $ratings[array_rand($ratings)];
24           $client = new App\Client($merchant);
25
26           $client->run();
27   }
```

For the abstractFactory method I copied the simulator.php code from the abstract factory pattern branch. I didn't organize the simulator code into classes, so I merely copied all the code into the method. That brings up a good point, though. Why did I copy all the code? If the code was already written in simulator.php, why didn't I require that file? I could have renamed each branch's simulator.php to the pattern name and then required the PHP script. I didn't do that because I think it is cleaner in this case to copy the code in each method of the facade. I say all this to bring us to the next point. Facades sometimes have their own code to implement in order to utilize the subsystem. Other times it may be as straightforward as calling some sequence of existing methods. In this case, you have to set up a few things before you eventually call the PatternExecutor.

app/PatternExecutor.php

```
30   public function adapter()
31   {
32           $crmAddress = with(new App\CRM\AddressLookup)->findByTelephone('555 867-5309');
33           $address = new App\CRM\AddressAdapter('Jenny Call', $crmAddress);
34           $mailClient = new App\MailClient;
35           $mailClient->sendLetter($address, 'Hello there, this is the body of
36           the letter');
37   }
```

The rest of the methods are left unlisted here. I think you probably understand how this facade is implemented now. Feel free to check out the git repository for other methods in the facade. Try implementing a few yourself if you're feeling really valiant!

Are Facades the Same as Adapters?

So, *how is a facade different from an adapter?* They are structured similarly. The fundamental difference is intent. The facade interface is not predetermined like the adapter interface. In an adapter, you can't name your methods willy-nilly because you have a client that expects a specific interface. The facade can name the methods whatever makes the most sense and hopefully whatever encourages the simplest usage for clients of the facade.

Furthermore, adapters aren't about taking complex layers and simplifying. They are about taking one layer and transforming it into another that the client already expects. Where the adapter pattern is analogous to an HDMI-to-DVI adapter, the facade pattern is much like having the HDMI output connected to a motherboard and its subcircuits. You don't need to know how the circuitry works together; you simply plug your cable into the HDMI interface and let the engineers worry about the underlying parts. In short, adapters convert layers, and facades hide them.

Conclusion

You saw in this chapter that you can use facades when you want to simplify some layer of code. A drawback to this pattern is that the facade is dependent on a wide variety of classes. If something changes in the underlying system, it can spell trouble for your facade. You may have to refactor the facade any time underlying changes to the subsystem are made. It also means that you need to understand how the low-level classes work together. Someone has to create and manage the facade. The benefits of having a facade means that all the developers on your team can take advantage of a simpler, easier-to-use API rather than having to deal with complexities of the lower subsystem.

Does a facade have to be a single class? Generally **yes**, a facade is usually a single class. You want your facade to be as straightforward as possible to use. If you create multiple classes, you need to know how those classes work together. A facade is already coupled with many modules from the subsystem, but you are hiding all of this from the client developer using the facade. This doesn't mean you have to create a giant super facade class. You could create multiple facade classes if it makes sense to break them apart and then you could also create another layer on top of those facades. A facade built on other facades. Just remember you want to keep it as simple as possible, and facades are more code that you have to manage. Consequently, when building a façade, make sure that the benefits outweigh the time it takes to build and manage the facade.

CHAPTER 14

Flyweight

```
$> git checkout flyweight
```

Intent

Use sharing to support large numbers of fine-grained objects efficiently.[1]

Applications

The flyweight pattern is used to reduce memory footprint. You will find this pattern helpful whenever you are dealing with a large number of objects that share the same properties or a few objects that share the same large size data (e.g. images). To illustrate, say you have a Person object that has properties like name, gender, and phone number. Assume the average memory cost for each Person object is 1,000 bytes. When you allocate 100,000 Person objects, you end up with 100 million bytes (95MB) of memory usage. Now let's also assume that all Person objects have the gender property set to "Female" and also assume that the string "Female" takes up roughly 300 bytes of memory. This means that you have roughly 300 x 100,000 bytes (28MB) of memory that is duplicated. (OMG, make it stop! NO MORE MATH PLZ!)

Bottom line: **taking advantage of shared data reduces your total memory consumption. Less memory likely means better performance.**

The Gang of Four calls data that can be shared between objects *intrinsic* and data that cannot be shared *extrinsic*. I find myself having to go back and remember which one is which. I'll save you the hassle and instead say the data is either *sharable* or *not sharable*.

How do you know what data is sharable? In the case of the Person class you had three properties: name, gender, and phone number. You might say that gender is sharable and name and phone number are not. Phone numbers and names are usually somewhat unique; however, what if in this application you are dealing with a data set that has a lot of duplicated names? In that case, you might save a significant amount of memory by making both name and gender sharable. It is up to you to determine what data is shared in the flyweight.

However, if you stop and think about it, in the traditional workflow of PHP, you likely won't need flyweights. What exactly do I mean by *traditional workflow of PHP*?

1. Some end user enters a URL into a browser to navigate to some route.

2. That route invokes the web server (Apache/Nginx) which in turn invokes PHP.

3. The PHP invokes operations such as database calls/business logic.

4. Eventually some HTML is served back to the end user over an HTTP protocol.

---

[1]*Design Patterns: Elements of Reusable Object-Oriented Software*, p. 218

K. Dockins, *Design Patterns in PHP and Laravel*, DOI 10.1007/978-1-4842-2451-9_14

All this is to say: **the life of a PHP script can be extremely short.** It takes time (about 15 seconds on my machine) to construct 100,000 objects. During this time your end user is impatiently tapping his foot waiting on the web page to respond. Not to mention that other users are also trying to request the same page. So the flyweight pattern doesn't make sense in a **stateless** request-response situation because it would take too long to construct lots of objects every time a route is requested.

Using the flyweight on a small collection of objects is probably overkill. So when would you use flyweight? Not all PHP falls under the request-response stateless HTTP paradigm. You can run PHP scripts on the command line. You can run PHP as a web socket service. You can even take advantage of Laravel's Queue[2] integration with Beanstalk and Amazon SQS to run PHP as background processes. Not every PHP script has to be run in mere milliseconds and thus there may be a time in which you want to use the flyweight pattern to save on memory. Now that I've shown why you might use the flyweight pattern, let's learn this pattern.

Abstract Structure

Figure 14-1 shows the structure.

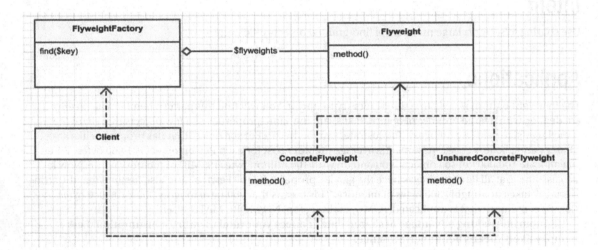

Figure 14-1. *The flyweight pattern*

- `Flyweight` is the base abstract class that all flyweight objects inherit from. If no base methods are needed, then this can just be an interface that the concrete flyweights implement.

- `FlyweightFactory` relieves the client of the burden of creating new flyweight objects. It handles the logic that determines when to create a new concrete flyweight object or point to an existing one that has been previously created. This factory contains an associative array, keeping track of all the created flyweights.

- `ConcreteFlyweight` is an instance of a `Flyweight`. It's properties are shared. It is important to remember that if a property is changed for this flyweight, it is changed for everyone who points to this flyweight. Shared flyweights should be treated as immutable, or else you jeopardize your sanity.

---

[2]`https://laravel.com/docs/master/queues`

- UnsharedConcreteFlyweight is an instance of an unshared flyweight. Sometimes you need to branch off and create a unique, unshared instance of a flyweight. Using the flyweight factory you create a special instance of the flyweight. This object is free to be changed at your will. One way you might do this is to create a clone method in your base Flyweight class. This way the flyweight factory can clone objects from existing objects and then cast them into an unshared flyweight. At that point, when you change any properties of the flyweight, you are not screwing with shared data. Sometimes you may not need this type of flyweight. It is only mentioned here to make you aware of the data sharing issue. I will illustrate this problem in the example.

Example

After days of researching different examples where other developers had used the flyweight pattern, I was discouraged. Many examples I saw were for game engines. In games, you're often dealing with bulky objects that share data. Worlds full of tanks and zombies. A forest full of trees. Particle blasts from a laser gun. You don't really do that kind of stuff in Laravel.

The Gang of Four used the flyweight pattern for a text editor. An image node repeated on a document shares the same memory for the image but contains non-shared image coordinates on the page. There is no need to duplicate the image data when only the positions differ. Web browsers do this same thing. Again, you don't really do this kind of stuff in Laravel either. Granted, you do use WYSIWYG editors but that has more to do with JavaScript than Laravel.

What is a good example to illustrate the flyweight pattern? This was a tough one for me. After thinking about this pattern for a while and still being stumped, I decided to watch some anime. I started with Nausicaa of the Valley of the Wind[3]. Still nothing; next was My Neighbor Totoro[4]. After finishing that, I watched Spirited Away[5]. At this point I'm desperate. Time to break out the big guns: Ponyo[6]. These things take **time**. *Time*, I thought, *there's a good example*. For example, when organizing appointments, you use dates on a calendar. You write down multiple appointments for the same date. You don't buy a five calendars just so you can write down five different appointments on the same day. You just write small in the box. Let's explore this concept further.

In this example, you will create a time-keeper flyweight which keeps a single date for a given day. You are going to load 100,000 users into your script, and each user has a last-logged-in date. To sweeten things up, most of your users have logged in within the last couple of months. You could create 100,000 date time objects, one for each user. However, you really only need about 60 date time objects that are collectively shared among users. To keep this example clean, you won't actually do anything with this mass of user objects. In reality, you'd actually *do something* with these 100,000 user objects you are spawning. You should also assume this script is run as some cron task, queue job, or one-off command line PHP script. As discussed earlier, you wouldn't likely load so many objects in a single network request.

Example Structure

Figure 14-2 shows the structure.

---

[3]http://en.wikipedia.org/wiki/Nausica%C3%A4_of_the_Valley_of_the_Wind_%28film%29
[4]http://en.wikipedia.org/wiki/My_Neighbor_Totoro
[5]http://en.wikipedia.org/wiki/Spirited_Away
[6]http://en.wikipedia.org/wiki/Ponyo

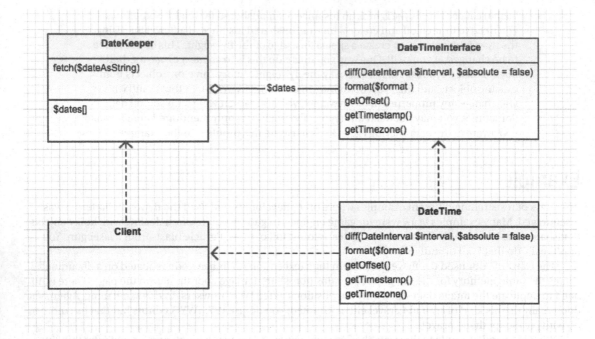

Figure 14-2. *The concrete example*

Implementation

Ahem... first a lesson on PHP and memory.

When I covered the prototype pattern (and cloning) I talked briefly about memory and pointers but let's cover this again in more detail. Why, you ask? If you understand how PHP allocates memory for variables, you should better understand how to implement the flyweight pattern. A couple of experiments will better explain how PHP allocates memory for variables. First off, I want to define a couple of things. A pointer is a small space in memory that simply points to the start of another memory address. It is analogous to forwarding an e-mail address (`pointer@stuff.com`) to another e-mail address (`real@stuff.com`). The data is all housed in the `real@stuff.com` inbox but you can still use both e-mail addresses. People smarter than me have stated the following:

> PHP is a dynamic, loosely typed language that uses copy-on-write and reference counting.[7]

What is reference counting[8]? It is the number of variables that reference a specific memory space. When the reference count reaches zero, then PHP internals know that they can discard the data in this memory space and reuse it for something else. Without reference counting you could not know when to deallocate memory. Eventually you would run out of memory. Using Xdebug, you can view the reference count for a variable. If you don't have Xdebug, use apt-get for Ubuntu, brew for Mac, or download the installer on Windows.

---

[7]http://PHP.net/manual/en/internals2.variables.intro.PHP
[8]http://PHP.net/manual/en/features.gc.refcounting-basics.PHP

app/memory/experiment1.php

```
$a = "hello there";
xdebug_debug_zval('a');
// a: (refcount=1, is_ref=0)='hello there'

$b = $a;
xdebug_debug_zval('a');
// a: (refcount=2, is_ref=0)='hello there'

$b = 'something else';
xdebug_debug_zval('a');
// a: (refcount=1, is_ref=0)='hello there'
```

Notice how the refcount increases when you assign $b to the variable $a? Internally, PHP did not create a new memory space for $b. It is faster this way (said people smarter than me). Later, when $b changes to something else, then you must allocate new memory, during which the refcount of $a goes back down to 1.

The next thing to address is what exactly **copy-on-write** means. When two or more variables are assigned to each other, they all share the same memory address. Only when one of those variables is altered does PHP duplicate the actual value in memory. You can see this in action using the memory_get_usage[9] function in your next experiment.

app/memory/experiment2.php

```
function print_member($step) {
        print "Step #{$step} - " . memory_get_usage() . PHP_EOL;
}
print_memory(1);                      // Step #1 - 226536 bytes
$a = array_fill(0, 200000, 0); // new memory allocated in Address#1
print_memory(2);                      // Step #2 - 19924088 bytes
$b = $a;                              // address of $b equ\
als address $a
print_memory(3);                      // Step #3 - 19924176 bytes
$b[4] = 4;                            // new memory allocat\
ed Address#2
print_memory(4);                      // Step #4 - 39621528 bytes
```

When you first start your program you are using 226,536 bytes. Okay, good. Who cares... **next step please!** In step 2, you allocate a huge array filled with 200,000 elements of value zero. In this step, you are now using 19,924,088 bytes of memory. That's a big increase! In step 3, when $b is assigned to $a you might expect to see the memory usage double but that doesn't happen. In fact, it only increases by 88 bytes. That is the amount of space needed to create a new pointer for $b and update the reference count in Address#1. Finally, when you alter $b in step 4 you see a huge difference in the memory usage because at this point when $b is altered you copied the memory from Address#1 into a new place, let's call it Address#2, and then you changed the fourth element of $b. This is how copy-on-write works. You don't copy memory values until the last possible moment when they are needed. That is why you can do something like the following code without running out of memory.

---

[9]http://PHP.net/manual/en/function.memory-get-usage.PHP

app/memory/experiment3.php

```php
$storage = [];
$a = array_fill(0, 200000, 'abc');

for ($i = 0; $i < 1000; $i++) {
        $storage[$i] = $a;
}

print $storage[999][3] . PHP_EOL; // abc
```

Notice above you are allocating 200,000 blocks inside array $a. According to your last experiment, 100,000 blocks was around 19,924,176 bytes, so if you double that it is close to 38MB of memory usage. If you looped this 1,000 times, that is almost 4GB of memory, which would grind most systems to a halt. The reason you don't crash and burn here is because of PHP's copy-on-write approach.

So far you've only dealt with strings, numbers, and arrays. How do objects behave? Objects still have reference counting and copy-on-write so they behave much in the same way. The following code illustrates a difference between objects and primitives.

app/memory/experiment4.php

```php
class SomeObject { public $answer; }

function change1($obj) { $obj->answer = 42; }
function change2($obj) { $obj = 'Douglas'; }

$x = new SomeObject();
$x->answer = 0;

change1($x);
change2($x);

var_dump($x);          // what is the output?
```

What is your output here?

1. Should you see your object with an answer of 0?

2. Should you see Douglas?

3. Should you see your answer has been changed to 42?

Turns out that the third option is correct, but why? Why does the answer property get changed to 42 in the change1 method, yet the change2 method has no effect at all? The answer lies in the fact that your object's properties are pointers referencing the same memory address. When you pass your $x to both change1 and change2 functions, you are creating a new memory pointer for $x itself, but all the properties of $x are still pointing to the same memory location. Thus, in change1 where you update $obj->answer = 42, that is changing the same memory address of $x->answer. In change2, when you update $obj = 'Douglas' you are changing a different memory address than that of $x. You will take advantage of this in your next experiment.

app/memory/experiment5.php

```php
$faker = Faker\Factory::create();
$faker->seed(42);
$storage = [];

$checkOne = memory_get_usage();

for ($i = 0; $i < 100000; $i++) {
        $storage[] = new Person($faker->firstName, $faker->boolean() ? 'Male' : 'Female');
}

$checkTwo = memory_get_usage();

print round(abs($checkTwo - $checkOne) / (1024*1024)) . 'MB memory'
. PHP_EOL;
// 44MB memory
```

The Faker[10] library provides you with pseudo-random first names and also random yes or no Boolean values to determine gender. You may need to run composer update to fetch Faker. You are creating a bunch of random Person objects in this experiment, and the total memory consumption is 44MB to store all 100,000 instances. Next, you are going to take advantage of what you found in experiment4. You decrease the amount of memory used by sharing the gender property across objects.

app/memory/experiment6.php

```php
$checkOne = memory_get_usage();

$male = new Gender('Male');
$female = new Gender('Female');

for ($i = 0; $i < 100000; $i++) {
        $storage[] = new Person($faker->firstName, $faker->boolean() ? $male : $female);
}

$checkTwo = memory_get_usage();

print round(abs($checkTwo - $checkOne) / (1024*1024)) . 'MB memory'
. PHP_EOL; // 39MB memory
```

So you saved 5MB of memory. That doesn't seem like a lot. In this case, you didn't save that much because the bulk of the memory usage is the person's name. Sharing the name property might save you even more space. I leave that as an exercise for you to try. Hopefully I've explained this concept of sharing data across memory in PHP in such a way that is understandable. But you haven't yet implemented the flyweight pattern. So far what you've done is called string interning[11]. Let's move on and implement your flyweight!

---

[10]https://github.com/fzaninotto/Faker
[11]http://en.wikipedia.org/wiki/String_interning

The Flyweight Implementation

When you use the flyweight pattern, you need a way to benchmark. The whole point of this pattern is to save on memory and enhance performance. If you don't know how much memory your program is using, then how can you know if all the work you put into making a flyweight *pays off*? You've already spent a good deal of this chapter on memory benchmarks, so you should be well acquainted with memory_get_usage, which is what you will be using to determine memory usage. Here is the simulator you will run to illustrate the flyweight. You will first see how much memory is used without the flyweight. Next, you will see how much memory you saved with the flyweight intact.

app/simulator.php

```php
$memory1 = memory_get_usage();
$time1 = microtime(true);

$people1 = [];

for ($i = 0; $i < 100000; $i++) {
        $person = new App\Person;
        $person->last_login = App\RandomDate::between('2014-11-01', '2014-12-01');
        $people1[] = $person;
}

$memory = round((memory_get_usage() - $memory1) / (1024 * 1024), 2);
$time = round(microtime(true) - $time1, 2);

print "Without flyweight, {$memory}MB of memory and {$time}s" . PHP_EOL;
```

The next step is to use a flyweight called DateKeeper to store dates. Unlike the previous code, dates from the DateKeeper are shared by the last_login property of the 100,000 Person objects created. In essence, you are repeating the code; the only major difference is you use the Flyweight factory when assigning a last_login date to the Person objects.

src/simulator.php

```php
$person->last_login = $dateKeeper->fetch(RandomDate::between('2014-11-01',
'2014-12-01'));
```

So what does the DateKeeper flyweight factory look like in this example? Let's check it out.

app/datekeeper.php

```php
class DateKeeper
{
        static private $dates = [];
        static public function fetch($dateAsString)
        {
                $datetime = is_a($dateAsString, 'DateTime') ? $dateAsString : new
\DateTime($dateAsString);

                $index = $datetime->format('Y-m-d');
```

```
        if (! array_key_exists($index, static::$dates)) {
                static::$dates[$index] = $datetime;
        }

        return static::$dates[$index];
    }
}
```

You might say, "oh, you're using statics; that's so *nasty!* Kelt!" Yeah, you're probably right. In this case, though, this gives you the advantage of not having to initialize a new DateKeeper. You can use this DateKeeper as sort of a simple singleton global everywhere! This might be really nifty if you wanted to use the DateKeeper in various places throughout your application without having to rely on the service container to make a singleton. That's really it. I wanted to point this out because you could also create the flyweight without static. When you don't use statics, you just need to make sure you pass the flyweight object around the application as needed or you lose all the cached objects and the benefits of the flyweight pattern.

As you can tell, this wasn't a whole lot of work to get your flyweight going. The flyweight shouldn't be a lot of work. Treat it for what it is: memory sharing.

Conclusion

To summarize, flyweight pattern is not a pattern you'll likely use in Laravel. Not to worry, though; this chapter wasn't a complete waste of time. You learned a lot about memory management in PHP. Knowing how memory is allocated in your PHP may seem too low-level but consider this. Pretend you pulled thousands of records from a database using Laravel's Eloquent ORM. You can take a little time and examine the memory usage and performance of this operation. Next, you can skip past the Eloquent ORM and go directly to using DB::table('table_name'). This approach would return stdClass objects instead of hydrating Eloquent models. It might be quicker and use less memory. I leave this as an exercise for you to try.

A drawback of the flyweight pattern is that it leads to more complicated code. It might not be worth the additional layer of complexity. You should always check to see how much memory is saved by using the flyweight. Sometimes the memory freedom gained is simply not worth the extra complexity of using a flyweight.

CHAPTER 15

Proxy

```
$> git checkout proxy
```

Intent

Provide a surrogate or placeholder for another object to control access to it.[1]

Applications

Proxies are the man-in-the-middle pattern. Instead of a client directly calling some object method, the incoming call first communicates with the proxy. Similar to a decorator, the proxy wraps itself around an object. Unlike the decorator, the proxy does not live to add new functionality to the wrapped object. So why do you use proxies? Why have a man in the middle? There are a few good reasons why you might do this and out of these reasons arise different types of proxies. These different types I'll list below, along with a reason why you'd want to use that type of proxy.

- **A virtual proxy** is used to delay construction of an underlying object or to simplify an object. When an object takes a while to load, you can use this proxy to construct an object only when it is absolutely needed. It can also be used to reduce complexity. For example, a method named doStuff could be more properly renamed to maximizeProfits through the use of a virtual proxy.

- **A remote proxy** is useful when you want to treat a remote resource as if it is local. Using a SOAP WSDL is an example but I have not used one of those in a long time. Many restful APIs, like Stripe, are accompanied by a library, which acts as a proxy to a web service.

- **A protection proxy** prevent access to methods. An UnauthenticatedProxy might not allow certain methods to its underlying delegate.

- **A smart proxy** adds additional functionality to a wrapped object. Firing an event or writing to a log file when an object method is invoked does not disturb the original object source code. This is similar to a decorator but you are not adding visible functionality to the object. The added functionality is transparent to the client.

There are other proxies but you'll have to discover them on your own. For now you will focus on these primary ones.

---

[1]*Design Patterns: Elements of Reusable Object-Oriented Software*, p. 233

K. Dockins, *Design Patterns in PHP and Laravel*, DOI 10.1007/978-1-4842-2451-9_15

Abstract Structure

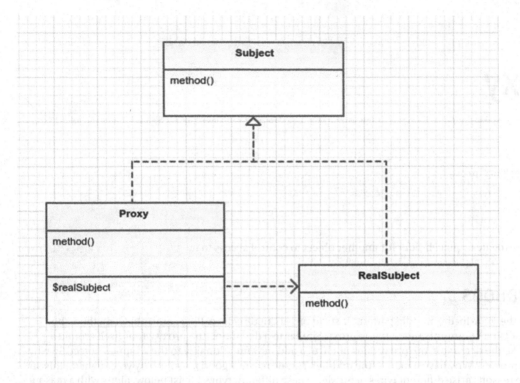

Figure 15-1. *The proxy pattern*

- Subject is an abstract class or interface that Proxy and RealSubject extend from. It defines the basic shared methods used. This is what you use when type hinting. See Figure 15-1.

- Real Subject is a concrete implementation of Subject. It will be used by the Proxy. The Proxy will generally wrap the Real Subject by composition.

- Proxy is used in place of a Real Subject. It is a surrogate for a Real Subject. If your vocabulary stinks like mine, then you probably hear the word surrogate and think about that movie with Bruce Willis. Therefore, allow me to define surrogate. A surrogate is a substitute. Similar to how a substitute teacher stands in for another teacher, the proxy will behave much like a real subject and only acts to substitute in features for protection, performance, or simplifying the Real Subject.

Example

In this example, you will create four different types of proxies.

- **Virtual proxy**: You will create a virtual proxy for a file reader. The file reader was designed to read a file and extract information from the file. When it constructs, it loads the file into memory. Your problem here is that you may be working with many of these file readers at once, and you don't want to load the file into memory unless you absolutely need to do so. See Figure 15-2.

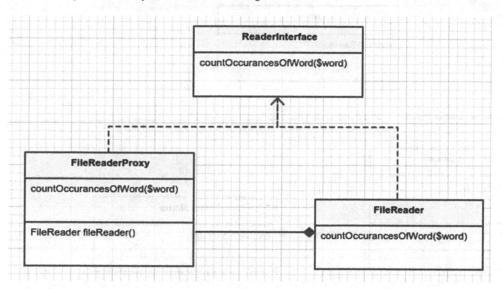

Figure 15-2. Virtual proxy - file reader

- **Remote proxy**: You have a remote restful API that you want to use. You will use Guzzle client to handle this. Your proxy will make it seem as if there is no restful API at all. This proxy hides the details of working with JSON and HTTP from your client. See Figure 15-3.

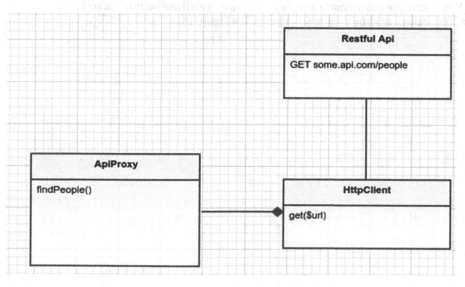

Figure 15-3. Remote proxy - fetching people

- **Protection proxy** : You have a gold mine that you want to mine. Some mines you can mine as much as you want. Other mines you want to restrict how much can be mined at any given time. You will use a protection proxy for this. See Figure 15-4.

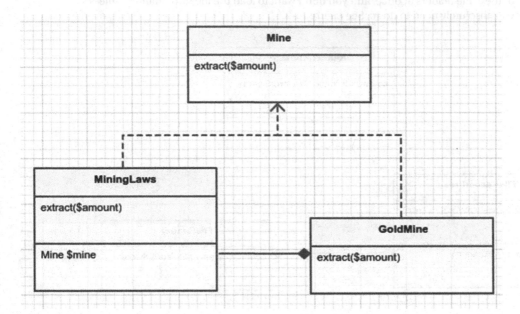

Figure 15-4. *Protection proxy - lawful mining*

- **Smart proxy**: Most miners keep to themselves. The don't want to share any information about their prized loot. Other miners can't keep their dirty mouths shut. These loudmouth miners have to boast and broadcast the amount of gold they mined. You'll simulate this scenario using a smart proxy. You'll use built-in Laravel events to broadcast when the mining takes place. See Figure 15-5.

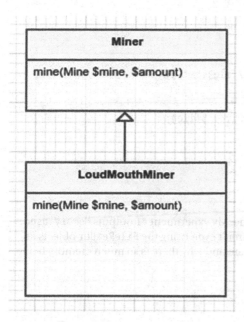

Figure 15-5. *Smart proxy - loudmouth miners*

Implementation

Virtual Proxy (Experiment 1 and 2)

A virtual proxy is used for constructing objects only when they are needed. In this example, you have a class called FileReader. The file reader loads a file into memory when it is first constructed. In cases where you have many different FileReader objects, you will consume a lot of memory. Sometimes you don't need to open the file until later. For example, if you have 100 file reader objects, you may only choose to operate with 10 of them. Therefore, holding those other 90 files in memory is a waste of resources. Your virtual proxy will delay construction of the FileReader until later.

In the first experiment, you'll see how much memory is used by the memory hog FileReader objects. This way you can compare how much memory you saved in the second experiment by using the virtual proxy.

app/experiment1.php

```php
$benchmark1 = memory_get_usage();
$baseDir = base_path();
$files = ['files/file1.txt', 'files/file2.txt', 'files/file3.txt'];

foreach ($files as $index => $file) {
        $files[$index] = new App\File\FileReader($baseDir . $file);
}

$benchmark2 = memory_get_usage();
$difference = $benchmark2 - $benchmark1;
print "Memory used: {$difference}" . PHP_EOL;
```

When you run this you might get a different number than me. My experiment #1 outputs `Memory used: 4373840`. That is roughly 4.2MB. It's important to note that you aren't even using the `FileReader` objects at this point. You only store three file readers into an array. To understand why there is so much memory being consumed, let's take a look at the actual `FileReader` class.

app/File/FileReader.php

```php
namespace App\File;

class FileReader implements ReaderInterface
{
        // somebody wrote this class so that it
        // loads a damn file when you construct... geesh
        public function __construct($path)
        {
                $this->file = file_get_contents($path);
                $this->path = $path;
        }
        public function countOccurancesOfWord($word)
        {
                return substr_count($this->file, $word);
        }
}
```

Why don't you refactor this file reader? Why not simply move `file_get_contents` out of the constructor? That would fix the problem. This class is quite simple, so it would be easy to refactor. However, two things. One is that not all classes are this simple. Two is that I want to demonstrate a virtual proxy. So stretch your imagination a little and just go with this example. Please? Thanks. I knew if I asked nicely you'd approve. In order to create a virtual proxy, you create a class cleverly called `FileReaderProxy`.

app/File/FileReaderProxy.php

```php
namespace App\File;

class FileReaderProxy implements ReaderInterface
{
        public function __construct($path)
        {
                $this->path = $path;
        }
```

```php
    public function countOccurancesOfWord($word)
    {
        return $this->fileReader()->countOccurancesOfWord();
    }
    protected function fileReader()
    {
        if (! $this->fileReader) {
            $this->fileReader = new FileReader($this->path);
        }
        return $this->fileReader;
    }
}
```

All this does is delay the creation of FileReader until countOccurancesOfWord is finally called. Although not practiced here, I could have initialize a new FileReader only to destroy it immediately after the count occurrences method finished. Reading from a file over and over might not be as effective as storing the file in memory until you are finished with it. In this case, you store the new file reader in an instance variable on the class so you can use it again later. I challenge you to try it the other way. Don't store the file reader and see how much memory is saved that way. Speaking of memory usage, let's run Experiment 2. Most of the code is the same except for a key difference.

app/experiment2.php

```php
foreach ($files as $index => $file) {
    $files[$index] = new \App\File\FileReaderProxy($baseDir . $file);
}
```

Running this experiment produces the output Memory used: 10552 (10KB). Using 10KB of space is a lot more effective than 4000KB of space. Granted, calling the countOccurancesOfWord method on all three files will use the same amount of memory. Why go through all this trouble? You make the assumption for this experiment that not every file will be loaded. You also reserve the right to alter your proxy and remove the file from memory each time you finish calling the countOccurancesOfWord method. This could help keep space free. That isn't the point of this exercise, though. The real point is understanding how virtual proxies allow you to change the performance of another class.

Remote Proxy (Experiment 3)

Remote proxies are useful when you have code running remotely but you want to treat it transparently as if it is running local. In this example, you create a proxy for a HTTP RESTful JSON service. You could call the web service directly. You could deal with JSON directly, too. The proxy can eliminate some of that complexity for you. This API you call finds a list of people. The people returned will have a paid or unpaid flag that you need. You will loop through and find all the people who have yet to pay their bill.

app/experiment3.php

```php
$api = new \App\Api\ApiProxy;
$people = $api->findPeople();

foreach ($people as $person) {
    if (! $person->paid) {
        print "{$person->name} has not paid yet!" . PHP_EOL;
    }
}
```

There is no mention of HTTP protocol or JSON anywhere in Experiment 3. Looking at this code, it would appear that everything here is run locally. The ApiProxy handles the delicacies of the HTTP client. For your HTTP client you use Guzzle because it is awesome to work with. You could set up a real server to communicate with but that's a lot of work. Instead, you make use of Guzzle's mocking ability to return mocked responses.

app/Api/MockedWebCalls.php

```php
use GuzzleHttp\Message\Response;
use GuzzleHttp\Stream\Stream;

$json = json_encode([
        ['id' => 1234, 'name' => 'John', 'paid' => false ],
        ['id' => 2345, 'name' => 'Joe', 'paid' => true ],
]);

$stream = Stream::factory($json);
$response = new Response(200);
$response->setBody($stream);

\App\Api\HttpClient::$mocks = [$response];
```

This mocking really has nothing to do with your remote proxy pattern, though. It is only mocking the response. When you first make a call to your HttpClient, it will return the encoded JSON string as the response with a status code of 200. Any additional calls made to your HttpClient will result in an exception being thrown. So far, this is Guzzle code. Let's take a look at your actual remote proxy.

app/Api/ApiProxy.php

```php
namespace App\Api;

class ApiProxy
{
        public function findPeople()
        {
                $client = new \App\Api\HttpClient;
                $response = $client->get('http://some.api.com/find/people');

                $peopleAsJson = $response->json();
                $people = [];

                foreach ($peopleAsJson as $personAsJson) {
                        $person = new App/Person;
                        $person->id = $personAsJson['id'];
                        $person->name = $personAsJson['name'];
                        $person->paid = $personAsJson['paid'];
                        $people[] = $person;
                }
                return $people;
        }
}
```

The ApiProxy fetches JSON data from the API server and converts it into an array of ApiPerson objects for you. In the case where you only pass data around, it probably isn't worth the overhead of creating Person objects. For now, let's assume you want more than just JSON. You want to go with classes that might have methods on them. Working with JSON objects in PHP does give you some structure to your data but it doesn't give you any class methods. Also, you can type hint and extend a class; you can't really do that with only JSON. The point of this example is to show how you've made it easier to work with a remote API by creating a proxy for it.

Protection Proxy (Experiment 4)

Sometimes you need to protect things. That is the protection proxy's job. In this example, you simulate a gold mine and miners. Each mine has a set amount of gold. The miners can mine the gold mine and continue to do so until a gold mine runs out of gold. There is a new sheriff in town and he says that no miner can mine over 500 ounces of gold per day. Let's see how this law can be applied as your protection proxy.

app/experiment4.php

```php
$miner = new \App\Mining\Miner('Big Bad John');
$goldmine = new \App\Mining\MiningLaws(new \App\Mining\Goldmine(10000));

// it is okay to mine a little bit at a time
$amount1 = $miner->mine($goldmine, 10); // mined 10
print "{$miner->name} attempts to mine 10 ounces and got $amount1" .
 PHP_EOL;

$amount2 = $miner->mine($goldmine, 50); // mined 50
print "{$miner->name} attempts to mine 50 ounces and got $amount2" .
 PHP_EOL;

$amount3 = $miner->mine($goldmine, 500); // only 100 due to mining 1
aws proxy
print "{$miner->name} attempts to mine 500 ounces and got $amount3"
. PHP_EOL;
```

In this example, you have mines and miners. Miners can mine, extracting out resources from the mine.

app/Mining/Miner.php

```php
namespace App\Mining;

class Miner
{
        public function __construct($name)
        {
                $this->name = $name;
        }
        public function mine(Mine $mine, $amount)
        {
                return $mine->extract($amount);
        }
}
```

Next, let's examine the gold mine class. It keeps track of how much gold is available to extract. Gold mines are initialized with a certain amount of available gold that can be extracted. They can't extract more gold than is available.

111

app/Mining/Goldmine.php

```php
namespace App\Mining;

class Goldmine implements Mine
{
        const TYPE = 'gold mine';

        protected $amountAvailable;

        public function __construct($amountAvailable)
        {
                $this->amountAvailable = $amountAvailable;
        }
        public function extract($amount)
        {
                if ($amount > $this->amountAvailable) {
                    $amount = $this->amountAvailable;
                }
                $this->amountAvailable -= $amount;

                return $amount;
        }
}
```

There is nothing in this class preventing a miner from mining more than 100 ounces of gold at a time. That is where your protection proxy comes in. In Experiment 4, a miner attempts to mine 10, 50, and 500 ounces of gold. You could place the conditional logic inside your Goldmine to not accept over 100 ounces of gold, but keeping the mining laws separate from the actual mine gives you more flexibility. It is flexible because it allows you to protect other types of mines and decouple the mining law from the actual gold mine. As another benefit, mining laws can be altered at runtime. So let's see how this mining law protection proxy works.

app/Mining/MiningLaws.php

```php
namespace App\Mining;

class MiningLaws implements Mine
{
        public function __construct(Mine $mine)
        {
                $this->Mine = $Mine;
        }

        public function extract($amount)
        {
                // limit to only 100 units at a time
                if ($amount > 100) {
                        $amount = 100;
                }

                return $this->mine->extract($amount);
        }
}
```

Protection proxies protect an underlying object. You're making use of composition instead of inheritance. You could have made MiningLaws extend Goldmine but in that case those laws would have been coupled to the gold mine. When you want to use other types of mines, such as a copper mine or coal mine, you could not reuse these same laws. That might be okay in some instances. Generally, however, it is easier to adapt to changes when you couple to interfaces, not concretions.

Speaking of things you could have done differently, why didn't you throw an exception here? The simple answer is because I wanted to draw your attention to it. Instead of changing the amount to 100, what if you had thrown a CallThePoliceException? It is good practice when dealing with permissions and protection proxies. *Throwing exceptions is a good practice period.* I leave this as an exercise for you to try if you'd like.

Smart Proxy

Sometimes you want to tack on additional functionality to an object. This is similar to a decorator. Where they differ is that the smart proxy generally hides its additional functionality under the public interface. The decorator could add additional new public methods, which a smart proxy probably wouldn't do. Let's add an event fire/broadcast to the miner application. The only thing that changes here is that when a miner mines something, you want an event to be triggered. Your smart proxy named LoudMouthMiner will handle this for you.

app/Mining/LoudMouthMiner.php

```php
namespace App\Mining;

class LoudMouthMining extends Miner
{
        public function __construct($name, Illuminate\Contracts\Events\Dispatcher = null)
        {
                parent::__construct($name);
                $this->event = $event ?: app('Illuminate\Contracts\Events\Dispatcher');
        }

        public function mine(Mine $mine, $amount)
        {
                $amount = parent::mine($mine, $amount);
                $this->event->fire('loud.mouth.mined', [$this, $mine, $amount]);
                return $amount;
        }
}
```

In the section about protection proxy I talked about using composition. Here you mix it up and use inheritance. You treat Miner like an abstract base class. While it is not named abstract, it is basic enough that all other miner types might extend from it. If you had other methods in your parent Miner class, you would not have to override them. The only thing this proxy does is add an event handler object, which is fired inside the mine method. Thus you don't need to use full composition because you don't need that much flexibility. Do what is easiest. If you are unsure about the Miner class and how much change it might incur, you might want to stick to composition because, like I said previously, it adapts easier with future changes.

Say you don't want to tack on fired events to different types of Miners that you might create. The way this code stands, it would be difficult. You would end up having to extend a LoudMouthMiner or writing duplicate code. A better approach would be to refactor and use composition. You could inject in a Miner type to the constructor and the LoudMouthMiner would no longer inherit from base class Miner. Enough about that. Let's look at Experiment 5.

app/experiment5.php

```
Event::listen('loud.mouth.mined', function (\App\Mining\Miner $miner, \App\Mining\Mine
$mine, $amount){
        print "{$miner->name} gone done mined {$amount} from the ol' " .
        $mine::TYPE . PHP_EOL;
});

$miner = new \App\Mining\LoudMouthMiner('Big Bad John');
$goldmine = new \App\Mining\Goldmine(10000);
$miner->mine($goldmine, 10);
```

Registering the event handler on Laravel's app will trigger this closure anytime the loud.mouth.mined event is fired. The anonymous function prints off the miner's name, the amount mined, and the type of mine. When you call the mine method on $miner, the event will be fired and handled. The loud mouth miner behaves much the same as the regular miner except that he fires an event internally. This is a smart proxy.

Conclusion

What are some of the drawbacks of the proxy pattern? One drawback is that it can sometimes be easier to refactor. In the case of your FileReader, you created another entire class that you have to manage just to work around the memory usage issue. A proxy is another class you have to maintain. You should be sure that it is worth the hassle.

Another drawback is that when you use composition you may write a lot of wrapper-like methods that call the underlying real subject. The proxy gives you two places to maintain the real subject code. You can get around this with inheritance but it means your base class could become more complicated.

Drawbacks aside, the proxy is a useful pattern to use when you want to substitute an object for another placeholder. Benefits of the proxy include performance gains, easier interfaces, and adding additional functionality.

CHAPTER 16

■ ■ ■

Chain of Responsibility

```
$> git checkout chain_of_responsibility
```

Intent

Avoid coupling the sender of a request to its receiver by giving more than one object a chance to handle the request. Chain the receiving objects and pass the request along the chain until an object handles it.[1]

Applications

Many things in life follow the Chain of Responsibility pattern: the military, businesses, and even casino slot machines. Take, for example, a call to your cell phone company's customer support. It usually starts with the automated voice system. If that doesn't satisfy you, then you are transferred to basic tier 1 support, and from there you manage to work your way up the tiers until you find yourself arguing with a tier 4 engineer. After a heated debate over frozen Popsicles, you request to speak to his manager.

Hopefully, at some point during this chain of command, your request is satisfied. If at any point during the process your phone disconnects, you'll have to start back at ground zero with the automated voice system.

Abstract Structure

- Client will call handleRequest on a specific instance of some Handler. At some point, the client's request is fulfilled and the client receives some request. See Figure 16-1.

- Handler is an abstract class or interface. All concrete handlers extend from the handler. All handlers may or may not have a successor. If the concrete handler is unable to handle the request, then the request is passed to his successor.

- ConcreteHandler1/ConcreteHandler2 actually implement the handleRequest method. Remember, though, that a handler does not necessarily handle a request. The request can be handed off to a successor that implements the Handler interface.

---

[1]*Design Patterns: Elements of Reusable Object-Oriented Software*, p. 251

© Kelt Dockins 2017
K. Dockins, *Design Patterns in PHP and Laravel*, DOI 10.1007/978-1-4842-2451-9_16

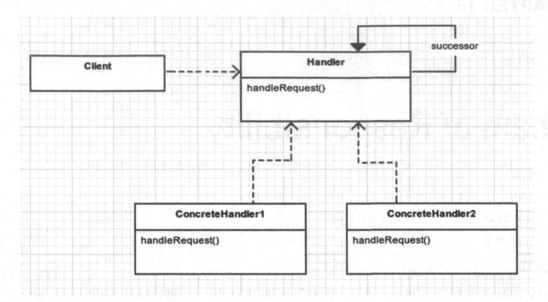

Figure 16-1. *Chain of responsibility pattern*

Example

It's a hard-knock life down on 37 Jump Street. The Big Bad Bird has the drug market cornered for a 20 block radius, and scoring is as simple as visiting Grouchy Oscar down by his trap can. I'm sure you are familiar with the different measurements of weed; however, for the sake of clarity let's list them here.

- Gram: The basic unit

- Eighth: 3.5 grams

- Quad: 7 grams

- Ounce: 28 grams

- Kilo: 1000 grams

A client will request a certain amount of marijuana. All requests begin with Grouchy Oscar. If a client's request is too high, Grouchy Oscar asks his boss to hook you up. If his boss can't satisfy your drug habit, he'll send you up the chain of dealers. This continues until no one is left. The Big Bad Bird is the head honcho so if you make it to him, then you're either throwing the world's biggest party or you're in some serious poop. To make it to The Big Bad Bird, you'll have to go through *AC Countant*. This guy is straight up numbers and business, and he isn't afraid to go guns a-blazing either. So be careful.

Grouchy Oscar will deal with various clients. One client even asks him for a cookie (guess who?). Since Oscar is just a simple street runner, he never deals out more than 3 grams to any client. In order to get more than 3 grams, you have to deal with Oscar's boss. His boss is Sniffy, who is an `EighthDealer` and will serve you only if your request is less than 7 grams; otherwise, you get to meet Sniffy's boss, who is a `QuadDealer`. Your request keeps going up the chain until satisfied.

Here are the rules you will define for each class:

- `GramDealers`: Serves no more than 3 grams

- `EighthDealers`: Serves no more than 7 grams

- QuadDealers: Serves no more than 28 grams
- OunceDealers: Serves no more than 1000 grams and narc protection
- KiloDealers: Narc protection

Example Structure

Figure 16-2 shows the structure.

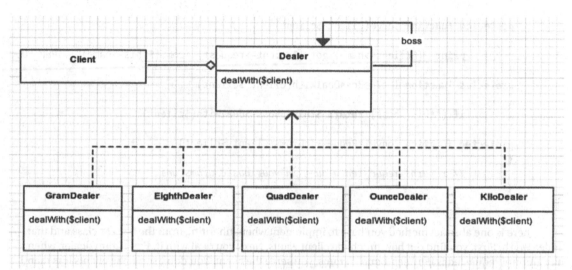

Figure 16-2. *Lots of dealing going on this street*

Implementation

The Dealer class has some basic helper methods in it. It is your base Handler abstract class that all concrete handlers will inherit from. The helper methods include serving the client, letting the boss deal with it, converting measurements into grams, and even shooting the client.

app/Dealer.php

```
namespace App;

abstract class Dealer;
{
        protected $boss;

        protected $name;

        abstract public function dealWith(Client $client);

        public function __construct($name)
        {
                $this->name = $name;
        }
```

```php
    public function boss(Dealer $dealer)
    {
            $this->boss = $dealer;
    }

    protected function shoot(Client $client)
    {
            print "{$client->name} got shot" . PHP_EOL;
    }

    protected function serve(Client $client)
    {
            print "{$client->name} got {$client->request} from {$this->name}" . PHP_EOL;
    }
    protected function letTheBossDealWith(Client $client)
    {
            if ($this->boss) return $this->boss->dealWith($client);
    }
    protected function convertRequestToGrams(Client $client)
    {
            // returns requested amount in your basic grams unit
    }
}
```

There is one abstract method you have to implement when inheriting from the Dealer class and that is dealWith. First, you find out how much the client wants. Next, you deal with it. For a gram dealer, when the amount requested is between 1 and 3 grams, you serve the client. You don't serve the clients less than 1 gram. Anything over 3 grams needs to be handled by your boss.

app/GramDealer.php

```php
namespace App;

class GramDealer extends Dealer
{
    public function dealWith(Client $client)
    {
            $amount = $this->convertRequestToGrams($client);

            if ($amount < 1) return;

            if ($amount > 3) return $this->letTheBossDealWith($client);

            return $this->serve($client);
    }
}
```

GramDealer, EighthDealer, QuadDealer, OunceDealer and KiloDealer all share the same interface, dealWith, and are very similar. They also rely on their boss in cases when they are unable to satisfy the client. In your simulation, Red Eye Mos is to get 2 grams from Oscar, EarnEz gets an ounce from Kabby, and so on.

app/simulator.php

```php
// create the dealers
$grouchyOscar = new \App\GramDealer('Grouchy Oscar');
$dealer2 = new \App\EighthDealer('Sniffy');
$dealer3 = new \App\QuadDealer('Kabby');
$dealer4 = new \App\OunceDealer('AC Countant');
$dealer5 = new \App\KiloDealer('The Big Bad Bird');

// setup the chain of responsibility
$grouchyOscar->boss($dealer2);
$dealer2->boss($dealer3);
$dealer3->boss($dealer4);
$dealer4->boss($dealer5);

// all deals start with Grouchy
$grouchyOscar->dealWith(new \App\Client('Red Eye Mos', '2 grams'));
$grouchyOscar->dealWith(new \App\Client('EarnEz', 'ounce'));
$grouchyOscar->dealWith(new \App\Client('Tellme Fatz', 'quad'));
$grouchyOscar->dealWith(new \App\Client('Cookie Hipster', 'cookie'));
$grouchyOscar->dealWith(new \App\Client('Zo 2 Easy', '99 grams'));
$grouchyOscar->dealWith(new \App\Client('Bertie', '4 eighths', $narc = tr\ue));
$grouchyOscar->dealWith(new \App\Client('Seth Rogen', '2 kilos'));

// Sniffy and Kabby are taken out of play
// because Bertie busted them
$grouchyOscar->boss($dealer4);

// Bertie the Narc gets greedy
// and gets shot
$grouchyOscar->dealWith(new Client('Bertie', 'kilo', $narc = true));
```

See how flexible this is? Grouchy even changes his boss in the middle of execution to the OunceDealer, *AC Countant*. In this particular simulation, you organized each dealer in a linear fashion, but the chain of responsibility allows you to be extremely flexible in swapping out successors without the need to alter a subclass. The chain keeps Sniffy's boss, Kabby, decoupled from Grouchy. That is important because on 37th Jump Street, dealers are busted or shot often. Being able to replace dealers dynamically at runtime keeps your program going. Imagine you had coupled each class. You would have something very inflexible. See Figure 16-3.

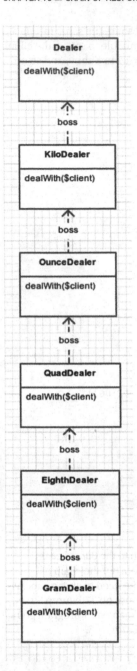

Figure 16-3. *Way too much inheritance, homie!*

This type of chained inheritance locks you into a set flow. You don't need this lock-in, especially when you might want to make a GramDealer skip past an EighthDealer and a QuadDealer go straight to an OunceDealer.

Conclusion

I like to think of the Chain of Responsibility pattern as the "call your boss when your customer is being a pain in the ass" pattern. Your boss makes more money than you for a reason, so let him deal with the bigger problems.

When using this pattern, you should be wary of circular references. Unless your application handles them, you could be heading for infinite loop-ville. Basically, in the following code, you are saying Oscar's boss is Sniffy and Sniffy's boss is Oscar, which doesn't make sense. The subordinate can't be the boss. This is why you spin into an infinite loop: the circular reference. This is a drawback of this pattern.

Dangerous Circular References

```
$grouchyOscar->boss($dealer2);
$dealer2->boss($grouchyOscar); // WAT?

$grouchyOscar->dealWith(new Client('Infinite Loop Man!', '2 grams');
 // Oscar handles this
$grouchyOscar->dealWith(new Client('Infinite Loop Man!', 'kilo');
// loopty loop forever!
```

The benefit of this pattern is that it allows you to decouple chains of requests. It is extremely flexible in that regard. For those of you who are computer science minded, you might see similarities in the chain of responsibility pattern and an object-oriented finite state machine where each state is terminal. However, technically a finite state machine can have multiple successors. The chain of responsibility pattern only has one successor. How do you know which successor to choose if you have multiple? Having only one successor means you don't have to worry about picking one. That limitation makes the chain pattern easier to work with than a finite state machine. If you find yourself needing a finite state machine, then check out the chapter about the **state pattern**.

You've seen how decoupling the requests into individual classes can help you be flexible with how you wire up and complete requests. It is a powerful pattern to use. Remember, however, that with great power comes evil aliens[2] and hobgoblins[3].

---

[2]http://en.wikipedia.org/wiki/Venom_%28comics%29
[3]http://en.wikipedia.org/wiki/Hobgoblin_%28comics%29

CHAPTER 17

Command

```
$> git checkout command
```

Intent

Encapsulate a request as an object, thereby letting you parameterize clients with different requests, queue or log requests, and support undoable operations. [1]

Applications

When you need to decouple an object that performs an action from an object that invokes an action, this is a good pattern to use. What does that last part really mean, though? Suppose you want to queue up a list of events that all do various different things. Later you will purge the queue, which will actually invoke all of those actions. Why would you not just invoke/perform the action immediately? There are some benefits to queuing some actions for a later time. One is that you can keep up with the sequential order that actions were invoked in. This allows you to have an *undo* feature. Another benefit is that you embody a request as an object. This makes customizing new requests as straightforward as creating a new command class.

Many real-world examples follow the command pattern. Take, for instance, a customer (a.k.a. a client) who orders his food. You can think of orders as commands. The waiter is the one who invokes the order. The cook receives the orders and creates a delicious dinner for the customer. See Figure 17-1.

---

[1]Design Patterns: Elements of Reusable Object-Oriented Software, p. 263

© Kelt Dockins 2017
K. Dockins, *Design Patterns in PHP and Laravel*, DOI 10.1007/978-1-4842-2451-9_17

123

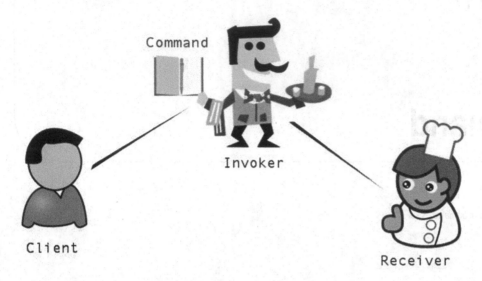

Figure 17-1. *Too many cooks (Clipart provided by openclipart.org.[2][3][4][5])*

Abstract Structure

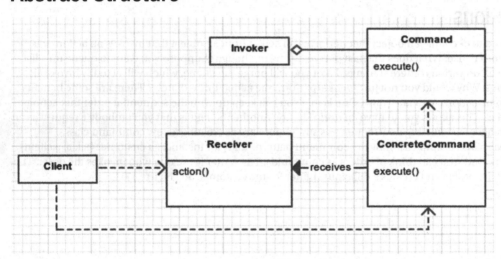

Figure 17-2. *Command pattern UML*

- Client creates the concrete command instances for use by the Invoker. See Figure 17-2.

- Receiver is the object a command will operate on. This could be a document, database, or any number of classes that hold the actual data you are performing commands on. The commands all operate on this receiver object.

---

[2]https://openclipart.org/detail/154837/people-cook-by-yyycatch
[3]https://openclipart.org/detail/77077/waiter-by-shokunin
[4]https://openclipart.org/detail/182377/notepadr-by-crisg-182377
[5]https://openclipart.org/detail/77077/waiter-by-shokunin

- **Command** is an abstract class that defines structure of all concrete commands.

- **ConcreteCommand** is a specific command classes. Although not a requirement, it often holds the ability to roll back actions. Commands operate on receivers.

- **Invoker** is what actually invokes a command. Say you are the client and the television is a receiver; the Invoker would be the remote control. Some possible commands invoked would be volume up and down.

Example

Instead of creating a contrived example, you are going to explore how migrations work within Laravel[6]. Migrations in Laravel were inspired by the Rails framework and provide a consistent way to create tables, columns, and indexes for a database. In addition to creating, migrations also provide rollback functionality in case you need to undo database changes.

Wait a minute. I thought this chapter was on the command pattern? Yes. Laravel migrations are an example of the command pattern found in the wild. I've taken the liberty of mapping the Laravel framework classes to the abstract UML diagram (Figure 17-2). So you are going to learn more about migrations and a new pattern! Talk about two dead birds. So you don't feel cheated, I'll also finish up the chapter with a simplified example of the command pattern using a television.

Example Structure

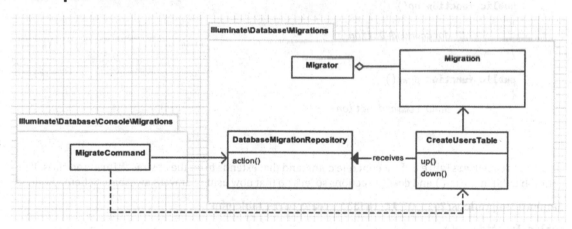

Figure 17-3. *Laravel migrations and the command pattern*

Figure 17-3 shows the structure.

Implementation

The first thing you are going to do is create a migration to create a users table in your database. You don't have a database set up, so for this example you will configure Laravel to use SQLite.

---

[6]http://laravel.com/docs/migrations

```
DB_CONNECTION=sqlite
```

If using SQLite, Laravel will attempt to use a database with the default name of database/database. sqlite. The user will need to create this file manually (i.e. using touch database/database.sqlite on the command line).

Ensure you have the SQLite driver enabled for PHP. On Ubuntu, this is as simple as sudo apt-get install php7.0-sqlite sqlite. If you don't want to use SQLite, feel free to use PgSQL or MySQL. You're using SQLite because it requires little effort to get set up.

If you look in the database/migrations folder you should notice a migration file for the users. It will have the timestamp attached to it, and the last part of the file name will be create_users_table. As a common good practice, you should name your migrations after the action you are performing. The name create_users_table clearly explains its purpose and action. What if you're not creating a table? What if you are adding a new field to an existing table? Then you could name your migration add_field1_to_users_table.

When naming migrations, be as specific as you can be.

Why does it even matter? It matters because you don't want to have two migrations called do_stuff; that is mega confusing, man. Each migration serves a purpose. Try to make that purpose clear in the file name.

Here is the file that was generated.

database/migrations/2014_07_11_185334_create_users_table.php

```php
class CreateUsersTable extends Migration
{
        public function up()
        {
                // do command action
        }

        public function down()
        {
                // undo command action
        }
}
```

The CreateUsersTable is the a concrete command that extends from the abstract Migration class. It's your job to fill in the up() and down() sections so let's do that now using Laravel's awesome Schema Builder[7].

database/migrations/2014_07_11_185334_create_users_table.php

```php
public function up()
{
        Schema::create('users', function ($table) {
                $table->increments('id');
                $table->string('first_name');
                $table->string('last_name');
                $table->string('email')->unique();
                $table->string('password');
                $table->timestamp('last_login_at')->nullable();
                $table->timestamps();                    // gives you created_at and updated_
        });
}
```

---

[7]http://laravel.com/docs/schema

```
public function down()
{
        Schema::drop('users');
}
```

There you go. You created a new users table with some fields: first_name, last_name, email, and so on. Let's run this bad boy!

php artisan migrate

With any luck you should see a message like the one below that lets you know that the migration command you created ran successfully. If not, make sure that your database is set up and configured correctly.

Migrated: 2014_07_11_185334_create_users_table

If you decide that you want to undo this migration, you can run php artisan migrate:rollback, which runs the down() method from your CreateUsersTable class and in turn drops the users table from the schema.

Notice that if you run php artisan migrate multiple consecutive times the script doesn't attempt to create the users table each time. Your pattern's invoker is called Migrator and it stores previously run migrations in a database table called migrations. You will take a look at Migrator in a moment; right now let's examine your pattern's client class: the MigrateCommand.

vendor/laravel/framework/src/Illuminate/Database/Console/Migrations/MigrateCommand.php

```
public function __construct(Migrator $migrator)
{
  parent::__construct();

  $this->migrator = $migrator;
}

public function fire()
{
  if (! $this->confirmToProceed()) {
      return;
  }

  $this->prepareDatabase();

  $this->migrator->run($this->getMigrationPaths(), [
      'pretend' => $this->option('pretend'),
      'step' => $this->option('step'),
  ]);

  foreach ($this->migrator->getNotes() as $note) {
      $this->output->writeln($note);
  }

  if ($this->option('seed')) {
      $this->call('db:seed', ['--force' => true]);
  }
}
```

vendor/laravel/framework/src/Illuminate/Database/Migrations/Migrator.php

```php
public function run($paths = [], array $options = [])
{
    $this->notes = [];
    $files = $this->getMigrationFiles($paths);
    $ran = $this->repository->getRan();
    $migrations = Collection::make($files)
                    ->reject(function ($file) use ($ran) {
                        return in_array($this->getMigrationName($file), $ran);
                    })->values()->all();
    $this->requireFiles($migrations);
    $this->runMigrationList($migrations, $options);
    return $migrations;
}

public function runMigrationList($migrations, array $options = [])
{
    if (count($migrations) == 0) {
        $this->note('<info>Nothing to migrate.</info>');
        return;
    }
    $batch = $this->repository->getNextBatchNumber();
    $pretend = Arr::get($options, 'pretend', false);
    $step = Arr::get($options, 'step', false);
    foreach ($migrations as $file) {
        $this->runUp($file, $batch, $pretend);
        if ($step) {
            $batch++;
        }
    }
}

protected function runUp($file, $batch, $pretend)
{
    $file = $this->getMigrationName($file);
    $migration = $this->resolve($file);
    if ($pretend) {
        return $this->pretendToRun($migration, 'up');
    }
    $this->runMigration($migration, 'up');
    $this->repository->log($file, $batch);
    $this->note("<info>Migrated:</info> {$file}");
}
```

The client utilizes the `Migrator` passed in the constructor and eventually runs the migrator. The key thing to pay attention to above is the `$this->migrator->run($paths = [], array $options = [])` method. This is what starts the `Invoker`. If you'd like to see how migrations are rolled back, there is another command called `RollbackCommand` you can look at. It uses the `Migrator` just like `MigrateCommand` does to call the `rollback` method instead of `run`.

The `Migrator` acts as the `Invoker` to run each migration command. But wait. Why does the `Client` know about the `Invoker`? I thought the client depended on the `Command` and `Receiver`? Is the UML diagram above wrong? Is this not really the command pattern? When you find patterns in the wild, they don't always match 1-to-I-don't-pretend-to-know-what-Taylor-Otwell-is-thinking. I doubt that the command pattern was at the forefront of his mind when he was writing this stuff. It is more likely that he was doing what felt right and this command pattern emerged. It is okay. You aren't the Pattern Police.

In fact, the way Taylor has written this, he has pretty much excluded a `Receiver` class. Don't let this deceive you, though, because in Laravel using what is called a facade[8] (not to be confused with the Facade pattern) lets you globally access many different parts of the framework from anywhere. In your `CreateUsersTable` the `Schema` builder assumes the role of `Receiver`.

How awesome is that? Imagine that before you ran any type of migration, you had to check to see if it had previous run before. Wouldn't that suck? Thankfully, all you have to worry about is filling in the `up()` and `down()` parts of each migration; the rest is on Laravel's handle. Migrations are generally used to alter the Schema but you are not limited. You could use `up()` to download photos from the Internet into the public/awesome-cat-photos directory. The `down()` command could simply delete the directory public/awesome-cat-photos.

It is important to point out that migrations are invoked in order. That is why there is a time stamp in the file name of each migration: to ensure that all migrations run in a specific chronological order. The command pattern also embraces chronological order. When you press Ctrl+Z in your text editor, it should undo the last thing you just did. Anything else would be frustrating.

The command pattern emerged to solve that exact problem: the undo button for a text editor! The authors did not want to couple command requests to the document itself. They used the document as a `Receiver` and the commands invoked upon the document object could easily be undone via the command pattern you just witnessed.

Television Command Pattern Example

In this short example, I will illustrate how the command pattern works using a television, remote control, and a hand. They say a picture is worth a 1,000 words. Whose counting though, amiright? Any who, here is a picture describing the situation you want to code out (see Figure 17-4).

---

[8]`http://laravel.com/docs/facades`

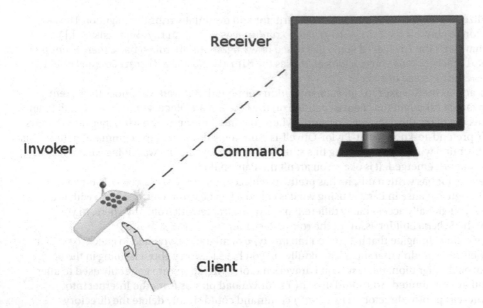

Figure 17-4. *Using the command pattern (clip art provided by openclipart.org)*

You are going to build a television remote that can execute commands but it also stores a history of commands that can be undone. Most television remotes don't store a history of commands. It's not a good user experience. If you hit the volume up button, it is better to hit the volume down button, not an undo button. In this case, you are building a spy remote. It will keep history of all commands sent. Why? Because you are a spy. Here is your remote control, which acts as the invoker.

app/Television/RemoteControl.php

```php
namespace App\Television;

class RemoteControl
{
        private $history;

        public function __construct()
        {
                $this->history = new \SplStack;
        }

        public function invoke(Command $command)
        {
                $this->history->push($command);
                $command->fire();
        }
}
```

You keep track of the history in a stack of command objects. Notice how the invoker knows nothing about what the actual command is doing, though. The invoker only fires commands and saves a history. You can add more functionality. You will provide a way to undo the commands.

app/Television/RemoteControl.php

```
public function undo($amount = 1)
{
        while ($amount-- > 0 && ! $this->history->isEmpty())
        {
                $command = $this->history->pop();

                $command->undo();
        }
}
```

This undo function pops commands off the stack and calls the undo method on the command. So what does a command look like? Here is a command that tackles changing volumes.

app/Television/ChangeVolume.php

```
namespace App\Television;

class ChangeVolume implements Command
{
        protected $tv;
        public function __construct(Television $tv, $delta = 1)
        {
                $this->tv = $tv;
                $this->delta = $delta;
        }

        public function fire()
        {
                $volume = $this->tv->getVolume();
                $this->tv->setVolume($volume + $this->delta);
        }

        public function undo()
        {
                $volume = $this->tv->getVolume();
                $this->tv->setVolume($volume - $this->delta);
        }
}
```

The command is initialized with a TV receiver object and a delta. Delta is an integer used to know how much the television volume should change each time this command is executed. Most commands are coupled to the receiver. You could make your receiver an interface, in case you wanted to be able to work with other concrete classes that implement the Television interface. In this example, though, you directly couple your commands to the receiver. Your receiver, the television, takes care of storing volume. It could store other properties, such as channel number, input source, video/audio settings. To keep this example simple, a television stores only volume.

131

app/Television/Television.php

```php
namespace App\Television;

class Television
{
    protected $volume;

    public function getVolume()
    {
        return $this->volume;
    }

    public function setVolume($volume)
    {
        if ($volume < 0) $volume = 0;
        if ($volume > 50) $volume = 50;
        $this->volume = $volume;
    }
}
```

Apart from acting as a model and storing volume, the Television class has some business logic to ensure no volume can be negative or over 50. Any sound over 50 would bust the speakers. You don't want busted speakers. The television class holds no knowledge about commands. At last, you put into action your client code. The first step of the client is to create the invoker, receiver, and command objects.

app/simulator.php

```php
$tv = new \App\Television\Television;
$control = new \App\Television\RemoteControl;
$volumeUp = new \App\Television\ChangeVolume($tv, 1);
$volumeUpFour = new \App\Television\ChangeVolume($tv, 4);
$volumeDown = new \App\Television\ChangeVolume($tv, -1);
```

Next, the client invokes the commands. I have commented beside each invocation method the change of the volume. This will come in handle later when you are undoing commands.

app/simulator.php

```php
$control->invoke($volumeUp);        // 1
$control->invoke($volumeUp);        // 2
$control->invoke($volumeDown);      // 1
$control->invoke($volumeUp);        // 2
$control->invoke($volumeUp);        // 3 <-- 6 more
$control->invoke($volumeDown);      // 2
$control->invoke($volumeUpFour);    // 6
$control->invoke($volumeUpFour);    // 10
$control->invoke($volumeUp);        // 11
$control->invoke($volumeUp);        // 12
$control->invoke($volumeUp);        // 13 <-- 4 ago
$control->invoke($volumeUp);        // 14
$control->invoke($volumeUp);        // 15
$control->invoke($volumeUp);        // 16
$control->invoke($volumeDown);      // 15 <-- current
```

You inspect the volume level at the current state. It should be at 15. Next, you roll back four commands and then six more, each time ensuring that you output the volume level. Those levels should be 13 and 3.

app/simulator.php

```
print $tv->getVolume() . PHP_EOL;  // 15
$control->undo(4);
print $tv->getVolume() . PHP_EOL;  // 13
$control->undo(6);
print $tv->getVolume() . PHP_EOL;  // 3
```

So there you have it. Another example of how the command pattern works. It is left to the client to construct and handle the invoker, receiver, and commands. The construction work could be delegated to factory named CreateRemoteControl.

Conclusion

The command pattern is great when dealing with requests that would be easier to work with if you treat them as objects. In these examples, you could write a big class that handles all commands for a television. You could write a large SQL file that handles the database. Doing so makes it difficult to work on specific sections of the code because you have a large block of code that represents all the commands. You encapsulate each command down into its own object. This means it is much easier to reuse commands and provide undoable actions as well.

The major disadvantage of the command pattern is the increase of classes to handle commands. The more classes you have, especially when classes differ widely, the easier it is to lose cohesion. When using migrations, you assume that all the classes you create are related to changing database structure. This doesn't have to be the case, though. You could use a migration to download pictures of Heidi Klum into the /public directory. That's a gross misuse of migrations but it is still technically possible. As long as you keep the purpose of the commands consistent, you shouldn't need to worry too much about overall cohesion.

Next, you'll learn about the interpreter pattern (see Figure 17-5).

Figure 17-5. *You've been beckoned.*

CHAPTER 18

███

Interpreter

```
$> git checkout interpreter
```

Intent

Given a language, define a representation for its grammar along with an interpreter that uses the representation to interpret sentences in the language.[1]

Applications

There are some patterns you might never use: flyweight, singleton, and this one. I am going to cover it anyway. Just in case. I have been wrong before. This chapter is a tad bit more theoretical than others. To understand the interpreter pattern, I need to talk first about language and grammar. Understanding how to work with grammar will make you sound more intelligent to others. This also happens to be the main benefit of the interpreter pattern.

Although this chapter may seem very theoretical, there are plenty of interpreters in the real world. The United Nations use hundreds of interpreters. You've probably used Google translate to interpret the Frozen song from English to Russian. That golden robot named C3PO has been programmed to translate over 6 million languages. Perhaps you've seen an American Sign Language interpreter waving their arms at the front of a stage.

Humans are natural interpreters. Even those who are uni-lingual and only speak English still interpret English sounds and words into meaning. This is where **context** matters. It is possible to derive different meanings from the same set of words. To illustrate the value of context, what is the meaning of *"I will get right on that?"* It depends on context. If your boss is asking for a TPS report, it probably means *"I will start working on the TPS report immediately."* However, if you change the context to your friend suggesting that you shave your entire body and pose naked on the Internet, your tone may be sarcastic and the meaning has changed to, *"Ha. Ha. I'm not doing that."* Same words. Different context equals different meaning. Hard is language, yes.

Sounding smarter is not the only application of the interpreter pattern. You can use the interpreter pattern when you want to translate domain-specific language into action. If your application deals with cars, then maybe you have certain mechanic *lingo* to translate. *Aftermarket* to a mechanic means parts not made by the original manufacturer. A *gas axe* is a cutting torch. *Wrenching* is slang for working on an engine. You want to use your mechanic vocabulary and an interpreter might be useful.

---

[1]*Design Patterns: Elements of Reusable Object-Oriented Software*, p. 274

© Kelt Dockins 2017
K. Dockins, *Design Patterns in PHP and Laravel*, DOI 10.1007/978-1-4842-2451-9_18

Context-Free Grammar

Why discuss context-free grammar? I want to show you what context-free grammar is so that you can use this nomenclature later in this chapter. I'm not trying to make your life harder, I promise.

Context-free grammar is a set of rules to generate patterns of strings. It consists of terminals and non-terminals. A non-terminal is composed of other non-terminals or terminals. A terminal is just a symbol. Imagine the language of $a's$ followed by b's and ending in a's. Some valid examples of this language would be

- aba

- aaaaba

- abaaaaaaa

- aabbaa

To represent the grammar for this language you will use Backus-Naur Form.[2]. You can read more about it on Wikipedia but you will likely understand how it works by just reading this next example.

```
<L> ::= <A><B><A>
<A> ::= 'a' | 'a' <A>
<B> ::= 'b'{<B>}
```

This might look strange at first. Non-terminals are wrapped in brackets, like < >. Symbols are wrapped in quotes, like ' '. The pipe (|) represents a choice; you can read it as or, meaning you can choose one side or the other. So in the case of <A> you can pick the symbol 'a' or 'a' followed by another 'a'. The non-terminal <A> uses recursion to build out a list of 'a' symbols. There is also a modified BNF syntax which I have used for <B>. The <B> rule works the same way as the <A> rule works. {<B>} means zero or more instances. You can write these grammars either way; it is up to your taste. I showed you both so you can take your pick.

What do you gain by writing your grammar in this BNF structure? When you write your grammar in this structure, you can easily tell where terminals and non-terminals are. A second benefit is that creating the code for this grammar is easier when you have a list of rules to abide by. A functional programmer would create a method for each non-terminal rule. Each method can call other non-terminal methods within the grammar. You will be doing something similar, except you will use classes instead of methods. Now that you know a little about grammar, you shall apply this knowledge in a bit.

Abstract Structure

- Client uses a global context and interpreter expressions to perform some set of actions. The set of actions that are executed (often on the context) depend on which expressions the client calls. The client can build the grammar using expressions. However, to avoid giving the client too much work, a parser class can handle building the grammar too. See Figure 18-1.

- GlobalContext is a class that holds global data available to all expressions. You can assign and look up variables in this class. If no shared data is needed, then you ignore this class.

- AbstractExpression is a base class/interface used by all terminal and non-terminal expressions. It contains the interpret method, which is defined specifically by all child classes.

---

[2]http://en.wikipedia.org/wiki/Backus%E2%80%93Naur_Form

- TerminalExpression implements the interpret method and does not rely on any other expressions. These are the expression rules with only 'strings' and no dependencies on other expressions.

- NonterminalExpression implements the interpret method and relies on other expressions. A non-terminal expression can easily be recursive if it depends on itself or depends on another expression that circles back around. You must try to prevent your grammar from having non-terminals that get stuck in some infinite recursion loop, never to finish. An application that loops indefinitely, never terminating and providing user feedback, is not useful.

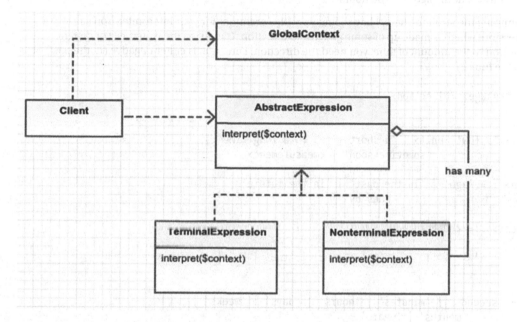

Figure 18-1. *Abstract structure*

Why do we make a distinction between non-terminal and terminal expressions? If you examine the code for a non-terminal and terminal expression class, they look pretty much the same. Both inherit from the base expression interface, so there isn't really a difference, code-wise. The only real difference is that a non-terminal expression has an extra attribute(s) to store other expressions. It might be worth a php-doc comment that states either non-terminal or terminal for each expression class. This allows you to quickly glance at the comments or even grep out all non-terminal expressions. Non-terminal expressions will be more difficult to troubleshoot than a terminal expression that has no further executions.

Example

I found a few examples on the Internet for this pattern.

1. Roman number translator

2. Reverse Polish calculator

3. Create your own SQL statements

These aren't things you likely do when building your web application. It was difficult to come up with an example, similar to the flyweight chapter, so I again relied on a time example. In this example, you will interpret certain phrases into a PHP date time. Here are a few candidate phrases you might need to interpret:

- "a few days ago" -> "- 3 days"

- "a short time in the future" -> "+ 10 minutes"

- "sometime soon" -> "+ 1 day"

- "a long time goes by" -> "+ 1 year"

- "fifty six hours ago" -> "- 56 hours"

By examining the structure here, I have come up with a grammar for your interpreter. You start with a time expression, which is made up of some gauge and direction. Gauge is a measurement or distance of time. In addition to the amount of time, you need the direction. Direction is either negative (in the past) or positive (in the future).

```
<time> ::= <gauge> <direction>


<gauge> ::= 'a few' <unit> | 'a short time' | 'a long time' |
                    'sometime soon' | <measurement>

<direction> ::= 'ago' | 'in the past' | 'in the future' |
                        'goes by' | ''

<measurement> ::= <number> <unit>

<number> ::= '1' | '2' | ... | '23' | 'one' | 'two' | ... | 'twenty \
three'

<unit> ::= 'seconds' | 'minutes' | 'hours' | 'days' | 'weeks' |
                'months' | 'years'
```

Ask yourself, is the gauge expression terminal or non-terminal? It is made up of a few literal strings but also expressions. That means it is non-terminal. Do you see which expressions? The unit and measurement expressions can potentially be part of a gauge expression. Notice that the direction expression is *terminal* because it links to no other expressions.

So why don't you just use regex or string replacements? For a small example, that could be easier. However, string matching can be unnerving as the complexity grows. Having a class to handle each type of expression makes it easier to understand what is going on. Each expression has its own job to do. It may take several expressions to finish the entire translation but you've broken each expression down into (hopefully) maintainable parts.

Example Structure

Figure 18-2 shows the structure.

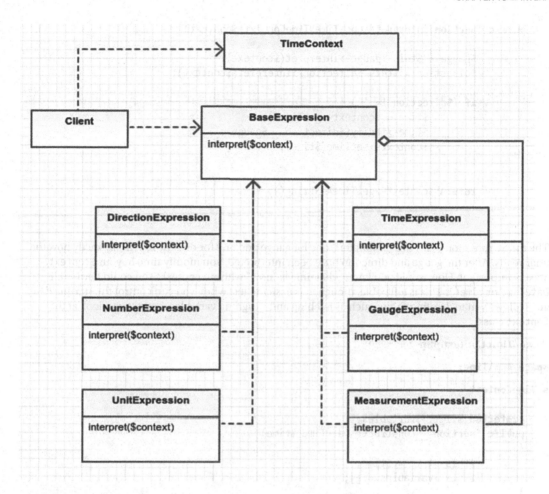

Figure 18-2. *Example structure*

Implementation

Believe it or not, the hard part is over. Earlier I came up with a set of BNF grammar rules. You create a class for each expression rule and follow the grammar to a tee. Let's make a class for the first expression, <time> ::= <gauge> <direction>.

app/Time/Expressions/TimeExpression.php

```php
namespace App\Time\Expressions;

class TimeExpression implements BaseExpression
{
        public function __construct(BaseExpression $gauge, BaseExpression
        $direction)
        {
                $this->gauge = $gauge;
                $this->direction = $direction;
        }
```

```php
    public function interpret(\App\Time\TimeContext $context)
    {
            $gauge = $this->gauge->interpret($context);
            $direction = $this->direction->interpret($context);

            if ($direction != '') {
                    $time = $context->getTime();
                    $time->modify($direction . $gauge);
                    $context->setTime($time);
            }

            return $context->getTimeAsString();
    }
}
```

The time expression takes two parameters, one for gauge and one for direction. This is exactly how the grammar reads. After the gauge and direction have been interpreted, you modify time in your $context. A context is important. How would you know what time is "now" without context? You could hard-code new DateTime or time(). This is inflexible, though. It is easier to test when you can control the starting date. A context allows you to do other things such as fetching and assigning variables. Let's have a look at the TimeContext class.

app/Time/TimeContext.php

namespace App\Time;

class TimeContext
```php
{
        protected $time, $variables;
        public function __construct(\DateTime $time)
        {
                $this->time = $time;
                $this->variables = [];
        }

        public function getTime()
        {
                return $this->time;
        }
        public function setTime(\DateTime $time)
        {
                $this->time = $time;
        }

        public function getTimeAsString($format = 'Y-m-d H:i:s')
        {
                return $this->time->format($format);
        }

        public function getVariable($key, $default = null)
        {
                return $this->hasVariable($key)
                    ? $this->variables[$key] : $default;
        }
}
```

```php
        public function setVariable($key, $value)
        {
                $this->variables[$key] = $value;
        }

        public function hasVariable($key)
        {
                return is_string($key)
                    && array_key_exists($key, $this->variables);
        }

        public function unsetVariable($key)
        {
                unset($this->variables[$key]);
        }
}
```

Why can you set variables on your context? I didn't make any mention of variables in the BNF, so what is a variable? You will get to that in just a second. First, let's look at another expression class, specifically the direction expression `<direction> ::= 'ago' | 'in the past' | 'in the future'`. It is a terminal expression because it does not rely on any other expressions.

app/Time/Expressions/DirectionExpression.php

namespace App\Time\Expressions;

class DirectionExpress implements BaseExpression
{

```php
        public function __construct($literal)
        {
                $this->literal = $literal;
        }

        public function interpret(\App\Time\TimeContext $context)
        {
                switch ($this->literal) {
                        case 'ago': return '-';
                        case 'in the past': return '-';
                        case 'in the future': return '+';
                        case 'goes by': return '+';
                        case '': return '+';
                }

                throw new \Exception('Could not interpret literal '
                            . $this->literal);
        }
}
```

The only responsibility the direction expression has is to return a '+' or '-'. A plus sign means in the future and a negative sign means in the past. This expression contains no outward calls to other expressions. Terminal expressions are nicer to work with than their non-terminal counterparts. Next up is the gauge expression, which should return an actual real measurement of time. The grammar rule looks like this:

```
<gauge> ::= 'a few' <unit> | 'a short time' | 'a long time' | 'sometime soon' |
<measurement>.
```

app/Time/Expressions/GaugeExpression.php

namespace App\Time\Expressions;

class GaugeExpression implements BaseExpression
```
{
        public function __construct($expr1, BaseExpression $expr2 = null)
        {
                $this->expr1 = $expr1;
                $this->expr2 = $expr2;
        }

        public function interpret(\App\Time\TimeContext $context)
        {
                if ($context->hasVariable($this->expr1)) {
                        return $context->getVariable($this->expr1);
                }
                switch ($this->expr1) {
                        case 'a few':
                          return '3 ' . $this->expr2->interpret
                          ($context);
                        case 'a short time':
                          return '10 minutes';

                        case 'a long time':
                          return '2 years';

                        case 'sometime soon':
                          return '1 day';
                }

                return $this->expr1->interpret($context);
        }
}
```

Switch gears back to the TimeContext and variables. Expressions like 'sometime soon' and 'a few' are relative. You want the flexibility of overriding those variables. Each literal has defaults, as you can see in the switch statement. The values can be overridden by the context, though. As I mentioned earlier, this is another benefit of having a context. Notice that if you don't find a literal expression, you assume the <measurement> rule is taking place and attempt to interpret that expression.

Next up, let's skip to the simulator (client) part. I could show you more expressions, but I think by now you've probably grasped the idea on expressions. You are free to browse the other expressions in the git repository. The simulator gives you an idea how to *put the pieces together*. Running the simulator client gives the following output:

```
$> php app/simulator.php

time for now:            2015-01-31 12:34:56
a few hours in the past: 2015-01-31 09:34:56
```

```
thirty days ago:        2015-01-01 09:34:56
sometime soon:          2015-01-01 09:44:56
a long time goes by:    2017-01-01 09:44:56
a short time ago:       2017-01-01 09:34:56
```

Let's look inside the simulator code for how this output is generated. In your application, all expressions need a context, thus you will need to initialize a `TimeContext`. For fun, you will reuse the same context throughout the execution the entire client.

app/simulator.php

```
1   $context = new TimeContext(new DateTime('2015-01-31 12:34:56'));
2   print "time for now:" . $context->getTimeAsString() . PHP_EOL;
```

Next, you put together a new time expression.

app/simulator.php

```
$gauge = new GaugeExpression('a few', new UnitExpression('hours'));
$direction = new DirectionExpression('in the past');
$time = new TimeExpression($gauge, $direction);
print "a few hours in the past: " . $time->interpret($context) . PHP_EOL;

// ... look in the git repository for more examples ...
```

And there you have it. Your first translation. It's not very pretty, eh? Even though you've done all this work, there is still a lot of work the client is forced to do. The client is responsible for setting up the context and the expressions, too. Geez, can't a client get a break? They sure can, and that is a great segue into the next section about a little parser that could.

Dude, Where's My Parser?

The client is not always responsible for wiring up the expressions. Sometimes you delegate that work to a parser. It would be nice to parse a string, instead of *stringing* together different expression classes. The parser is not originally part of the interpreter pattern. Don't be sad, my friend; you are going to make a parser anyway. This will give you an idea of how you might put the interpreter expressions and parser together. Let's rewrite your simulator code from above and add some syntax sugar.

app/simulator-with-parser.php

```
print "a few hours in the past: " . $parser->interpret('a few hours
in the past', $context) . PHP_EOL;
```

Ah, that's nice, right? No more hard-coding a new `TimeExpression` into the client code. You only need to call the parser's interpreter with a string and context object. So how does this parser work underneath the hood? Each parser can vary. Each parser can be dramatically different. The basic idea I follow is this.

1. Break apart the sentence into an array of tokens.

2. Move a cursor to the first token.

3. Match/identify the token with a grammar rule.

4.   Keep moving the cursor forward to the next token.

5.   Keep going until you process all the tokens.

So **what is a token?** In your case, you will split the sentence into an array of single words. However, a token could also be a single character. You don't need such granularity in your parser, though.

What is a cursor? The cursor is an integer that points to the current index of your tokens array. This pointer helps you keep up with the tokens you have already processed. The cursor allows you to move forward or even backwards for some parsers. As soon as you identify a token, you advance the cursor forward. When the cursor reaches the end of the tokens array, you should be finished parsing the string. If an error occurs, you can use the cursor position inside an exception to broadcast the issue for troubleshooting by the developer or client. You see this kind of behavior when you leave out semicolons and make mistakes in your code. It makes it easier to track down errors when you have a line number and a stack trace. You aren't going to such extravagant measures as including stack tracing but the principle is still here if you wanted to extend your parser to include more debugging options.

app/Time/TimeParser.php

```php
class TimeExpressionParser
{
        protected $tokens, $cursor;

        public function __construct(NumberParser $numberParser)
        {
                $this->numberParser = $numberParser;
        }

        public function interpret($sentence, $context)
        {
                return $this->parse($sentence)->interpret($context);
        }
```

You have protected attributes to keep up with the token array and the current processed token cursor position within the array. The construction of a parser relies on a number parser. The NumberParser transforms strings like "sixty five" into the digits "65". You could expand on this parser but there is no need because I just said what it does.

The interpret method seems fairly harmless. It parses the sentence and then runs the interpret method on the interpreter object that was returned. So let's dig in further and look at the parse method.

app/Time/TimeParser.php

```php
public function parse($sentence)
{
        $this->tokens = explode(' ', $sentence);

        $this->cursor = 0;

        $gauge = $this->gauge();

        $direction = $this->direction();

        return new Expressions\TimeExpression($gauge, $direction);
}
```

The parse method handles spitting the sentence into tokens. You want to start at the beginning of your tokens array so you set the cursor position to zero. Next, you have two helper methods that fetch the gauge and direction expressions. Finally, you return a new time expression. Let's take a look at how you fetch the gauge expression.

app/Time/TimeParser.php

```php
protected function gauge()
{
    $section = $this->tokens(2);

    if ($section == 'a few') {

        $this->cursor += 2;

        $unit = new Expressions\UnitExpression($this->tokens(1));

        $this->cursor += 1;

        return new Expressions\GaugeExpression($section, $unit);
    }
    if ($section == 'sometime soon') {

        $this->cursor += 2;

        return new Expressions\GaugeExpression($section);

    }

    $section = $this->tokens(3);

    if ($section == 'a short time' || $section == 'a long time') {

        $this->cursor += 3;

        return new Expressions\GaugeExpression($section);
    }

    $measurement = $this->measurement();

    return new Expressions\GaugeExpression($measurement);
}
```

Whew, there's a lot going on in that method. Each condition returns a GaugeExpression, so you can almost look at this method as one giant switch statement. Recall the rules for <gauge>:

```
<gauge> ::= 'a few' <unit> | 'a short time' | 'a long time' | 'some\
time soon' | <measurement>
```

Each condition in your gauge method is checking for the tokens you find within your expression grammar. Let's take a look at the very first conditional matching 'a few'.

app/Time/TimeParser.php

```
if ($section == 'a few') {
        $this->cursor += 2;

        $unit = new Expressions\UnitExpression($this->tokens(1));

        $this->cursor += 1;

        return new Expressions\GaugeExpression($section, $unit);
}
```

When you match the tokens 'a few' you will need to advance the cursor two spots because 'a few' is two words. Next, you take advantage of the fact that 'units' are only one word, so whatever the next word is must be your unit. Of course, you could be dealing with invalid syntax. You assume `UnitExpression` will throw an exception if the unit token you provide is invalid. After advancing the token one more spot, you return the new gauge expression. I could cover the `direction` method but I think by now you can see how to use tokens and a cursor to strip out words that make up your expressions. Notice that you are still using the same expression classes and grammar. Before you manually created expression classes inside of the `simulator. php`. Now your parser is creating the new expression objects for you. The parser has nothing to do with the interpreter pattern, though. It is merely an expression factory that creates the objects using the grammar and interpreter pattern you already built earlier.

Parsers are usually built custom for grammar and syntax rules. Every parser differs. Some grammars will be harder to parse than others. I outlined some guidelines above, such as using a tokens array and a cursor, to help you build your own parser. The basic takeaway idea here is that you can reuse your grammar from your interpreter pattern inside your parser.

Conclusion

You've seen how the interpreter pattern helped translate a phrase into a date-time. You also built a parser to integrate a string and interpreter expressions. Turning each grammar rule into classes helps keep your code maintainable and easier to understand. If you want to further extend your grammar, you only need to add more expression classes.

Adding more expression classes can be a downside, too. These expression classes all work together. If one expression fails to do its job correctly, then it could throw off all the other expressions. Even though each expression may be straightforward, the expressions all work together. The expressions can have nested dependencies on each other, making it difficult to trace through an interweaving tangle. This is why each component needs to be thoroughly tested.

In your example, you created a parser. As the grammar grows, the parser that creates your interpreters can challenge you too. You are managing the grammar in two places: the parser and the interpreters. A parser needs to be heavily tested to ensure that it creates the correct interpretation expressions. It is coupled tightly to expressions, which can cause a headache if the underlying rules of the expressions change later.

The interpreter pattern has also been rumored to be slow. Slower than what, though? A full blown parser? A machine learning algorithm? I haven't seen any real benchmarks or evidence of this claim. My hunch is that, yes, this pattern will be slower than some hand-crafted algorithm. Chances are you may never use this design pattern, but at least now you know the basics of how it works.

CHAPTER 19

■ ■ ■

Iterator

```
$> git checkout iterator
```

Intent

Provide a way to access the elements of an aggregate object sequentially without exposing its underlying representation.[1]

Applications

What is an aggregate object? The word aggregate means *a whole formed by combining several elements*. In programming terms, it's a collection, array, list, etc. Why use an aggregate object, though? You can already aggregate a bunch of numbers, strings, or objects all sequentially using arrays. Why do you need the iterator pattern? Is this a useless pattern? The answer is no.

There are some benefits you gain from using an iterator object. The first benefit is that the mechanisms used by the iterator to traverse from one item to the next time are all hidden. You don't have to expose the guts of how you get from point A to Z. The client uses the same interface for all the iterators and doesn't have to worry about keeping up with some counter index within a for loop. The client just keeps asking for the next item until the iterator no longer provides any more. This is different than the traditional way of stepping through arrays, and it provides much more flexibility.

The next major benefit of an iterator is that you can easily change the order of items in your aggregate object by switching the iterator object. The iterator is responsible for traversing the list in a specific order. Perhaps you want to shuffle your list or filter out items that meet a search criteria or even traverse backwards over the list. This is where the iterator pattern really shines.

Imagine you have a bunch of songs on your iPod/iPhone/Droid phone. If you're anything like me, the order in which these songs play matters. I don't want to hear Marvin Gaye followed by Rage Against the Machine. Or maybe I do; it depends on my mood. Some days I want to hear new pop music. Other times I want to listen to older songs. Some days I want a random cocktail mixture of music. I can never have too much Justin Bieber and his father, Bob Seger[2], in the mix. You have the ability to arrange your collection of songs using a playlist.

In this sense, playlists are synonymous with iterators. Playlists determine the order of songs. The songs know nothing about their order. That's what playlists are for. So if playlists are the iterator, then what would be the aggregate object? In this analogy, that would probably be you, since you are creating the playlist and own all of the songs. The aggregate object is the thing that constructs the iterator. You will learn more about this soon.

---

[1]*Design Patterns: Elements of Reusable Object-Oriented Software*, p. 289
[2]`www.bobseger.com/`

© Kelt Dockins 2017
K. Dockins, *Design Patterns in PHP and Laravel*, DOI 10.1007/978-1-4842-2451-9_19

Abstract Structure

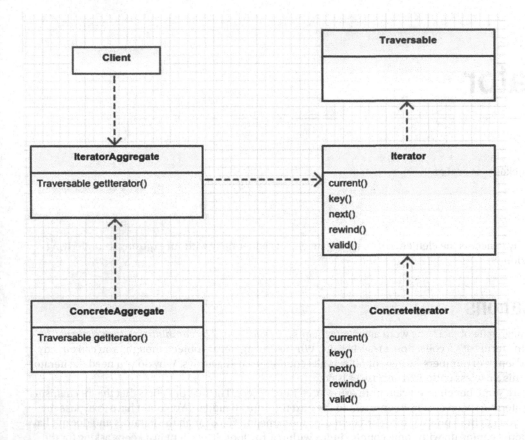

Figure 19-1. *Abstract structure*

■ **Note** PHP internal interfaces/classes are outlined in red.

- IteratorAggregate is the abstract PHP internal interface[3] for an aggregate object. The getIterator method of this interface is meant to be defined by the ConcreteAggregate. The method should generate new Iterator objects. Note that if you need additional methods besides the getIterator method, then you could create your own base iterator interface that extends from this interface. See Figure 19-1.

---

[3]http://php.net/manual/en/class.iteratoraggregate.php

- **Iterator** is the abstract PHP internal interface[4] that contains methods required to traverse over a list.

  - current() returns the current active element.

  - key() returns the index of the current active element.

  - next() moves forward to the next element.

  - rewind() moves the iterator to the first element.

  - valid() checks to see if you are at the end of the iterator.

- Traversable is an abstract empty interface and is treated specially by PHP[5]. Its purpose is to allow you the flexibility to use your iterators inside a foreach loop. You will see more on this later in this chapter. The Iterator interface inherits from this abstract interface by default so you don't have to worry much about it. It is worth mentioning so you understand how PHP iterators work. For now, just know that without this interface you would not have the convenience of using your iterators inside foreach.

- ConcreteAggregate holds the actual implementation of the getIterator method. It also contains a reference to an array, list, or collection of items. It will need to pass its items to the constructor of the Iterator objects that are generated.

- ConcreteIterator is an actual implementation of the Iterator interface. There are some built-in PHP concrete iterators[6]. You will be using ArrayIterator[7] in your example.

Example

In this example, you are going to create a list of movies. You will iterate over this collection of movies using your different iterators. The iterators are created by the aggregate object, Movies, in this scenario. After you have furthered your understanding of the iterator pattern, you will finish the chapter by looking at how Laravel uses the iterator pattern in its own neat way for Eloquent collections.

---

[4]http://php.net/manual/en/class.iterator.php
[5]http://php.net/manual/en/class.traversable.php
[6]http://php.net/manual/en/spl.iterators.php
[7]http://php.net/manual/en/class.arrayiterator.php

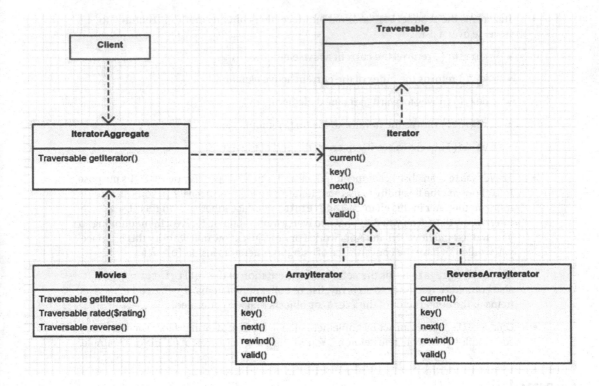

Figure 19-2. *Example structure*

Example Structure

 Note that there are two concrete iterators listed in Figure 19-2. I just wanted to show you how easy it is to create an iterator in PHP that traverses an array backwards.

Implementation

First, you need a Movie object to store the title and rating of your movie. Nothing special going on here, and this isn't even part of the iterator pattern.

app/Movie.php

```php
namespace App;

class Movie
{
        protected $title, $rating;

        public function __construct($title, $rating)
        {
                $this->title = $title;
```

```
            $this->rating = $rating;
    }

    public function title()
    {
            return $this->title;
    }

    public function rating()
    {
            return $this->rating;
    }
}
```

Next comes your aggregate iterator. You need a way to add movies.

app/Movies.php

```
namespace App;

class Movies implements \IteratorAggregate
{
        protected $list = [];

        public function add(Movie $movie)
        {
                $this->list[] = $movie;
        }
```

Remember this is the class that generates iterator objects. You have three iterators being created inside this class so let's look at them all in closer detail. The first one is the default getIterator method and it generates a new ArrayIterator using your movie list.

app/Movies.php

```
12    public function getIterator()
13    {
14            return new \ArrayIterator($this->list);
15    }
```

Next, you create an iterator that acts as a filter on the movie rating. You use the ArrayIterator to accomplish this.

app/Movies.php

```
17    public function rated($rating)
18    {
19            $filtered = array_filter($this->list, function ($item) use ($rating) {
20
21                    return $item->rating() === $rating;
22            });
23
24            return new \ArrayIterator($filtered);
25    }
```

151

You've probably guessed by now that the ArrayIterator is a pretty useful iterator. Next, you are going to generate a knock-off version of this iterator called ReverseArrayIterator. This iterator doesn't exist out of the box in PHP so you will have to create it soon.

app/Movies.php

```
27    public function reverse()
28    {
29              return new ReverseArrayIterator($this->list);
30    }
```

As promised, here is the ReverseArrayIterator. You could make your own implementation of current, key, next, rewind, valid; however, it is easier to reverse the array and then piggy-back off of ArrayIterator. Once again, ArrayIterator to your rescue.

app/ReverseArrayIterator.php

```
class ReverseArrayIterator extends \ArrayIterator
{
        public function __construct(array $array)
        {
                parent::__construct(array_reverse($array));
        }
}
```

So you've covered a couple of classes. Now it is time to see this thing in action. The whole point of all this work is to keep details about traversing the list of items hidden from the client. Let's see if you've done that or not. First, your client must add a list of movies. I'll show that here; try not to laugh too hard.

app/simulator.php

```
$movies = new \App\Movies;
$movies->add(new \App\Movie('Ponyo', 'G'));
$movies->add(new \App\Movie('Kill Bill', 'R'));
$movies->add(new \App\Movie('The Santa Clause', 'PG'));
$movies->add(new \App\Movie('Guardians of the Galaxy', 'PG-13'));
$movies->add(new \App\Movie('Reservoir dogs', 'R'));
$movies->add(new \App\Movie('Sharknado', 'PG-13'));
$movies->add(new \App\Movie('Back to the Future', 'PG'));
```

Now comes the moment of truth. You want to loop over these movies in three different ways. The first way is the normal way, which uses getIterator and foreach. This will use the ArrayIterator and spit out all the movies added to your movies aggregate object.

app/simulator.php

```
print 'MOVIE LISTING' . PHP_EOL;

foreach ($movies as $movie) {
        print ' - ' . $movie->title() . PHP_EOL;
}
```

For those of you with eagle eyes, you might be wondering where the call to getIterator is made. To those of you I say, congratulations, you get a sticker[8]! If you didn't get a sticker, then maybe you already know the trick? It is a bit of PHP magic. Earlier I mentioned the special Traversable interface. This interface is used only with IteratorAggregate or Iterator. In your case, Movies extends from IteratorAggregate so it is also extending Traversable. That is how PHP knows to magically use the getIterator method in the above code without you explicitly calling it. Try to think of this as a convenience to keep your code prettier, not some magical unicorn feature.

In the next bit of code you will have to be explicit and call your iterator methods by their name. You get one freebie magic show. Now it's time to be **unequivocal.** (I knew this thesaurus I got for Christmas would come in handy.)

app/simulator.php

```php
print PHP_EOL . 'RATED R ONLY' . PHP_EOL;

foreach ($movies->rated('R') as $movie) {
        print ' - ' . $movie->title() . PHP_EOL;
}
```

You will do the same with your reverse iterator.

app/simulator.php

```php
print PHP_EOL . 'IN REVERSE ORDER' . PHP_EOL;


foreach ($movies->reverse() as $movie) {
        print ' - ' . $movie->title() . PHP_EOL;
}
```

Notice how throughout all of this, you did not have to keep up with indexes, filtering, or ordering. It was all done for you behind the scenes. The client is still responsible for calling the iterator. The client is not responsible for details on how to get to the next item. Although you know it is an array driving the iterators behind the curtain, the client does not. There is nothing preventing you from swapping out the array in Movies with something else, say a List, and your client code should still function the same.

Laravel Collections

Now that you have an idea of how iterators work, let's explore Laravel. Laravel has something called collections. It uses collections with its ORM called Eloquent. The database retrieval workflow is something like this:

1. Build database query using the Eloquent query builder (also known as Fluent).

2. Execute the query. For selects, table rows are retrieved.

3. Fields from each table row are *hydrated* into Model.

4. Each Model is added to an Eloquent collection.

5. The collection is returned.

---

[8]Sticker not provided by me; sorry, I have no stickers to give out. You'll have to ask the sticker man for your sticker. Do you know the sticker man?

Eloquent collections in Laravel are a nice wrapper around Models. If you're interested, you can check out the file at vendor/laravel/framework/src/Illuminate/Database/Eloquent/Collection.php. The Eloquent collection extends a base generic *support* collection. This nifty class can be found in Illuminate\Support\Collection and has over 1,300 lines of helper methods. It also has nothing to do with databases, so you can use it for any type of data structures. You are interested in this class to see how it uses the iterator pattern.

vendor/laravel/framework/src/Illuminate/Support/Collection.php

```
12   class Collection implements ArrayAccess, Arrayable, Countable, IteratorAggregate,
13   Jsonable, JsonSerializable {
14
15        use Macroable;
16
17        /**
18         * The items contained in the collection.
19         *
20         * @var array
21         */
22        protected $items = [];
23
24        /**
25         * Create a new collection.
26         *
27         * @param array $items
28         * @return void
29         */
30        public function __construct(array $items = [])
31        {
32                $this->items = $items;
33        }
```

This class implements a lot of other stuff; nonetheless, it still implements IteratorAggregate, which is exactly how the Movies class you created works. There should be a getIterator method inside here.

vendor/laravel/framework/src/Illuminate/Support/Collection.php

```
610   public function getIterator()
611   {
612           return new ArrayIterator($this->items);
613   }
```

That is kind of boring, though. You've already seen this exact thing done earlier in your Movies aggregate object. But wait! Below this getIterator line there is something new:

vendor/laravel/framework/src/Illuminate/Support/Collection.php

```
620   public function getCachingIterator($flags = CachingIterator::CALL_TO
621   STRING)
622   {
623           return new CachingIterator($this->getIterator(), $flags);
624   }
```

Remember that list I showed you earlier[9] with all the built-in native PHP iterators? CachingIterator[10] is another built-in iterator you can use. Why would you use it?

What does it do? The PHP docs don't offer much insight stating only, *This object supports cached iterator over another Iterator*. What good does it do you to cache another iterator? There is one really good use case I've found for this iterator and it is when you need to **look ahead** during your traversal. Imagine you need to know the next item in the traversal and do some logic based on that. Below you will do just that.

app/cache-example.php

```
$numbers = new CachingIterator(new ArrayIterator([1, 2, 3, 1, 4, 6, 3, 9]));

foreach ($numbers as $currentNumber) {
        $sign = '';
        if ($numbers->hasNext()) {
                $nextNumber = $numbers->getInnerIterator()->current();
                $sign = $nextNumber > $currentNumber ? '>' : '<';
        }

        print $sign ? "$currentNumber $sign " : $currentNumber;
}

print PHP_EOL;
```

In this example, you should expect the following output:

```
B> 1 > 2 > 3 < 1 > 4 > 6 < 3 > 9
```

This all works because you can look ahead. Without the caching iterator you would not be able to look ahead to see if the next number is greater than or less than the current number. There are plenty of other useful iterators, such as RecursiveDirectoryIterator[11] and AppendIterator[12]. I encourage you to investigate those. By now you have covered enough iterators. I'm tired, amigo.

Conclusion

At the end of each chapter I try to list the downsides to each pattern. One downside of the iterator pattern is that there are five methods you must define in order to create your own custom iterator. This might seem overwhelming. Why do you need to have a hasNext() method? What should key() return? These are questions you'll have to answer if you end up creating some custom iterator rather than relying on native PHP SPL iterators.

The upside to the iterator pattern is that you hide details about how to traverse objects. That is the intent. No longer are you forced to use for loops with integer indexes. You can loop over complex lists and trees. Also, much like you did for the rating filter in your Movies class, you can easily create methods that return special filtered iterators. This takes the work load off the client.

You learned a lot about iterators in PHP. Try to use as much out-of-the-box SPL stuff as possible. One downside is that the documentation is lacking. However, that shouldn't stop you from using the iterator pattern whenever you find yourself dealing with collections of objects. In Laravel, you will use collections quite often, and Taylor has done a lot of work to handle iterating and array-like access on collections. Take a good look around the Collection class; it has some neat methods in there that are also undocumented but very useful!

---

[9]http://php.net/manual/en/spl.iterators.php
[10]http://php.net/manual/en/class.cachingiterator.php
[11]http://php.net/manual/en/class.recursivedirectoryiterator.php
[12]http://php.net/manual/en/class.appenditerator.php

CHAPTER 20

■ ■ ■

Mediator

```
$> git checkout mediator
$> composer update
```

Intent

Define an object that encapsulates how a set of objects interact. Mediator promotes loose coupling by keeping objects from referring to each other explicitly, and it lets you vary their interaction independently.[1]

Applications

Everyone needs help sometimes. Sometimes you have enough on your plate. The mediator is that guy in the middle who works with you. A few examples of real-world mediators are lawyers, secretaries, and real estate agents. The real estate agent works with the buyer and seller to accomplish the task of changing ownership of a home. Typically, the buyer and seller never communicate directly; all communication flows through the real estate agent.

The Gang of Four book lists user interface controls as an example use case for the mediator pattern. What is a user interface control? Imagine you are looking at a drop-down box and a Save button. Until you select a valid option from the drop-down box, the Save button is disabled. These two widgets don't need to know about each other. The Save button only needs to know if it is enabled or not. A mediator can help with this.

However, you aren't building user interfaces in Java or Smalltalk. You use Laravel. You write HTML, which is served as a view to the client. Granted, there may be JavaScript/jQuery handling the disabling/enabling feature of the Save button but at that point you are outside the context of Laravel. Therefore, using the mediator pattern to communicate between user interface controls *inside Laravel views* is not something you will do.

Abstract Structure

- `AbstractMediator` is an interface or abstract class. Its methods are implemented by the concrete mediator. The abstract methods laid out here will be the public API for colleagues to notify the mediator. See Figure 20-1.

- `Mediator` contains methods used by the concrete colleagues. These methods can notify other colleagues or do whatever they need.

---

[1] *Design Patterns: Elements of Reusable Object-Oriented Software*, p. 305

© Kelt Dockins 2017
K. Dockins, *Design Patterns in PHP and Laravel*, DOI 10.1007/978-1-4842-2451-9_20

- `AbstractColleague` is an interface or abstract class. This abstract class can hold methods used by all colleague objects and also hold a reference to the mediator object.

- `Colleague1` and `Colleague2` are implementations of the `AbstractColleague`. Each colleague does not know about the other's existence. If these colleagues ever communicate directly to each other, it defeats the purpose of the mediator pattern.

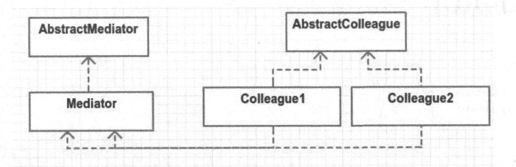

Figure 20-1. *Abstract structure*

Example

In this example, you are going to build the beginnings of an e-commerce checkout system. If you've ever built or managed e-commerce then you know how painful it can be. Money always complicates things. In this platform, you are going to rely on a price adjuster mediator. The adjuster holds business logic for calculating price adjustments. You have products, customer benefits, and coupons. The price adjuster recalculates product prices based on the customer benefits and coupons you add to the system. So when you add a coupon for *block cheese* you should automatically see the block cheese **product** price change, all thanks to the mediator that handles price adjusting. Just as a general workflow, this is what you want:

- Customer adds a few products.

- Product prices automatically change as customer adds (or removes) coupons and benefits.

I am going to define two abstract ideas here: **price adjustments** and the **price adjuster**. The price adjuster (mediator) takes all of its price adjustments (colleagues) into consideration when tallying up the prices.

⚠ **Just as a warning**, I'm not recommending the mediator pattern for e-commerce, but it seemed like a good example to showcase this pattern. Business logic for pricing can be terrible to work with, especially when strung out across many, many files. Many factors can affect pricing, things like how many products you are ordering, coupons, what country you live in, if you're a veteran or over 65 or if you love a good apple. Okay, that last one probably never gets used but I do love a good apple.

In this example, you also have an arbitrary business rule that customers lose benefits if using three or more coupons. Why three or more? I don't know. Go ask the client. It's important, ya know?

Example Structure

Figure 20-2 shows the structure.

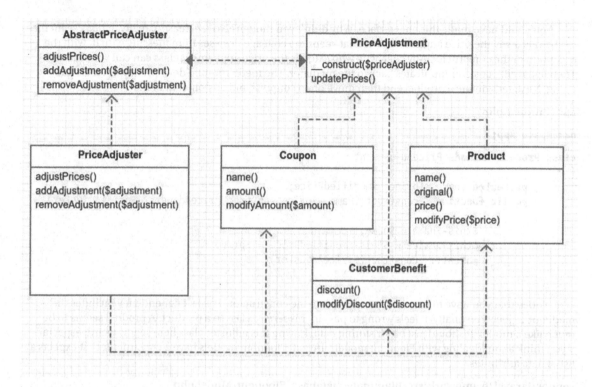

Figure 20-2. *Example structure*

Implementation

The abstract price adjustment class takes the role of your abstract colleague. It's primary goal is to set the price adjuster and then update prices using that price adjuster mediator object. This class is extended by products, coupons, and customer benefits.

src/PriceAdjustment.php

```php
abstract class PriceAdjustment
{
    private $priceAdjuster;

    protected function __construct(AbstractPriceAdjuster $priceAdjuster)
    {
        $this->priceAdjuster = $priceAdjuster;
        $this->priceAdjuster->addAdjustment($this);
    }
    protected function updatePrices()
```

```
        {
                $this->priceAdjuster->adjustPrices($this);
        }
}
```

You could have made this an interface. Why didn't you though? No *real* reason, really. It does seem nice to abstract away the price adjuster object. That keeps the colleague classes from messing with it, with the exception of the constructor. Any colleague who extends the price adjustment class can call updatePrices. Then updatePrices communicates back to the mediator. The mediator then does whatever it feels like doing. Next, let's define a product and then move on to coupons and customer benefits.

app/Product.php

```
namespace App;

class Product extends PriceAdjustment
{
        protected $name, $price, $modifiedPrice;
        public function __construct($name, $price, AbstractPriceAdjuster $priceAdjuster)
        {
                $this->name = $name;
                $this->price = $this->modifiedPrice = $price;
                parent::__construct($priceAdjuster);
        }
```

Notice that you have to pass in dependencies to the constructor. The last dependency includes the mediator object. Personally, it feels wrong to pass in this *service* class to a product. A product seems to be much like a model. It should just be for storing data. Having this adjuster class here seems weird, especially if you think about dealing with Eloquent models. In fact, Eloquent models have a constructor that expects a list of data attributes.

vendor/laravel/framework/src/Illuminate/Database/Eloquent/Model.php

```
public function __construct(array $attributes = []) {
...
}
```

You'd be going against the grain if you tried to inject this extra mediator class into an Eloquent model. A pattern that fits Eloquent models better is the observer pattern. In fact, Eloquent has the observer pattern baked in already. I will cover that in a few chapters. Getting back to products, you see that the rest of the methods are accessors and mutators.

src/Product.php

```
15    public function name()
16    {
17            return $this->name;
18    }
19
20    public function original()
21    {
22            return $this->price;
23    }
24
```

```
25    public function price()
26    {
27            return $this->modifiedPrice;
28    }
29
30    public function modifyPrice($price)
31    {
32            $this->modifiedPrice = $price;
33            $this->updatePrices();
34    }
```

Take note that anytime you modify the product price, you need to call updatePrices. This method calls the price adjuster mediator, which takes care of the prices for you. It is nice to have price calculations separate from the actual product class. Next, take a look at coupons and customer benefits. These classes are very similar to your Product class.

app/Coupon.php

namespace App;

class Coupon extends PriceAdjustment
```
{
        protected $name, $amount;

        public function __construct($name, $amount, AbstractPriceAdjuster $priceAdjuster)
        {
                $this->name = $name;
                $this->amount = $amount;
                parent::__construct($priceAdjuster);
        }

        // name() and amount() accessors omitted
        public function modifyAmount($amount)
        {
                $this->amount = $amount;
                $this->updatePrices();
        }
}
```

Again, when you modify the amount of a coupon, you need to tell the price adjuster to update prices. You will do the same whenever a customer benefit discount is modified.

app/CustomerBenefit.php

namespace App;

class CustomerBenefit extends PriceAdjustment
```
{
        protected $discount;

        public function construct($discount, AbstractPriceAdjuster $priceAdjuster)
        {
                if ($discount > 100) throw new Exception("cannot have a discount over 100%");

                $this->discount = $discount;

                parent:: construct($priceAdjuster);
        }
```

```
        // discount() accessor omitted

    public function modifyDiscount($discount)
    {
            $this->discount = $discount;
            $this->updatePrices();
    }
}
```

It might seem weird to you that coupon and customer benefits can change. In real life, a coupon doesn't generally change price. And if it does, it would likely just be treated as a totally different coupon. A coupon is much like a value object. Value objects should be treated as immutable. The reason why is outside of the scope of this chapter but a Google search[2] can fill you in if you are curious. However, in this example, you are allowing coupons and benefits to be changed after they are created, instead of treating them as immutable value objects.

So far you've got your price adjustment classes squared away. The next step is making the price adjuster. I'm not going to show the abstract price adjuster[3] here because it is just an interface and you can easily see which methods it needs implemented in the above UML diagram. Let's skip straight to the meat: the price adjuster mediator.

app/PriceAdjuster.php

```
namespace App;

use Illuminate\Support\Collection;

class PriceAdjuster implements AbstractPriceAdjuster
{
        protected $cid = 1;

        public function construct()
        {
                $this->products = new Collection;
                $this->coupons = new Collection;
                $this->customerBenefits = new Collection;
                $this->appliedCoupons = [];
        }
```

You construct the price adjuster with three new collections and an array. As part of your business rules, you can only apply one coupon per product. This is why you have an array for applied coupons. Next, you enter the heart of this mediator: adjustPrices.

app/PriceAdjuster.php

```
17    public function adjustPrices()
18    {
19            $customerDiscount = $this->getCustomerDiscount();
20
21            foreach ($this->products as $product) {
22                    $oldPrice = $product->price();
```

---

[2]www.google.com/webhp#q=why%20should%20value%20objects%20be%20immutable
[3]https://github.com/kdocki/larasign/blob/mediator/src/AbstractPriceAdjuster.php

```
23              $newPrice = round($this->getCouponDiscountForProduct($product) *
24              1 - $customerDiscount / 100), 2);
25              if ($oldPrice !== $newPrice) $product->modifyPrice($newPrice);
26          }
27  }
```

This method loops through all your products and finds a coupon discount for the product and then subtracts the customer discount. If the math confuses you, don't worry; it just means you're not 21 anymore. The condition that compares oldPrice to newPrice is very important. Besides not needing to update a product's price if it hasn't changed, this condition keeps you from recursively calling yourself over and over. Remember when you modify a product's price, it then calls the price adjuster. This would keep calling itself over and over, and you would get an annoying *Maximum recursion depth exceeded* stack trace. Continuing on, you still need to implement two more methods that take care of adding and removing adjustments.

app/PriceAdjuster.php

```
27  public function addAdjustment(PriceAdjustment $adjustment)
28  {
29          $this->{'add' . get_class($adjustment)}($adjustment);
30  }
31
32  public function removeAdjustment(PriceAdjustment $adjustment)
33  {
34          $this->{'remove' . get_class($adjustment)}($adjustment);
35  }
36
37  protected function addProduct(Product $product)
38  {
39          $this->addToCollection($this->products, $product);
40  }
41
42  protected function addCustomerBenefit(CustomerBenefit $benefit)
43  {
44          $this->addToCollection($this->customerBenefits, $benefit);
45  }
46
47  protected function addCoupon(Coupon $coupon)
48  {
49          $this->addToCollection($this->coupons, $coupon);
50  }
51
52  protected function removeProduct(Product $product)
53  {
54          unset($this->appliedCoupons[$product->cid]);
55          $this->removeFromCollection($this->products, $product);
56  }
57
58  protected function removeCoupon(Coupon $coupon)
59  {
60          $key = array_search($coupon->cid, $this->appliedCoupons);
61
62          if ($key !== false) unset($this->appliedCoupons[$key]);
63
```

```
64              $this->removeFromCollection($this->coupons, $coupon);
65      }
66
67      protected function removeCustomerBenefit(CustomerBenefit $benefit)
68      {
69              $this->removeFromCollection($this->customerBenefits, $benefit);
70      }
71
72      protected function addToCollection($collection, $object)
73      {
74              $object->cid = $this->cid++;
75
76              $collection->push($object);
77
78              $this->adjustPrices();
79      }
80
81      protected function removeFromCollection($collection, $object)
82      {
83              $key = $collection->search($object);
84
85              $collection->forget($key);
86
87              $this->adjustPrices();
88      }
```

There are a few more protected methods in the price adjuster but they don't really have anything to do with the mediator pattern. If you're curious about the rest of this class, please do check out the code on GitHub[4].

Now it is finally time to run this bad boy! In your simulation, you will add a few products and coupons and even a customer discount. You will then print off the prices of your products and the total price too. The simulator looks like this:

app/simulator.php

```
6     $priceAdjuster = new \App\PriceAdjuster;
7
8     $product1 = new \App\Product('Block Cheese', 3.99, $priceAdjuster);
9     $product2 = new Product('Frozen Pizza', 6.69, $priceAdjuster);
10    $product3 = new Product('Popcorn', 2.34, $priceAdjuster);
11    price()('untouched prices', $product1, $product2, $product3);
```

Here you are creating three new products and setting names and prices. The price method gives you the following output:

```
--- untouched prices ---
Block Cheese: 3.99
Frozen Pizza: 6.69
Popcorn: 2.34
total: 13.02
```

---

[4]https://github.com/kdocki/larasign/blob/mediator/src/PriceAdjuster.php

These virgin prices have not been adjusted by your adjuster yet. Let's change that by adding a few coupons.

app/simulator.php

```
13    $coupon1 = new \App\Coupon('Block Cheese', 1.00, $priceAdjuster);
14    $coupon2 = new Coupon('Frozen Pizza', 2.00, $priceAdjuster);
15    price('adding 2 coupons', $product1, $product2, $product3);
```

Now that the coupons have been added, the price adjuster does its thing. You can see that block cheese and frozen pizza is cheaper now.

```
--- adding 2 coupons ---
Block Cheese: 2.99
Frozen Pizza: 4.69
Popcorn: 2.34
total: 10.02
```

Next, you get your customer benefit, which discounts your price 30%. Again, by adding the price adjuster to the class the prices are automatically adjusted.

app/simulator.php

```
17    $benefit1 = new \App\CustomerBenefit(30, $priceAdjuster);
18    price('added 30% customer benefit', $product1, $product2, $product3);
```

```
--- added 30% customer benefit ---
Block Cheese: 2.09
Frozen Pizza: 3.28
Popcorn: 1.64
total: 7.01
```

Remember that as part of your business rules described above, the customer loses his or her benefits if using more than two coupons.

app/simulator.php

```
13    $coupon3 = new Coupon('Popcorn', 2.00, $priceAdjuster);
14    price('adding 3rd coupon, customer looses 30% benefit', $product1,
15    $product2, $product3);
```

```
--- adding 3rd coupon, customer looses 30% benefit ---
Block Cheese: 2.99
Frozen Pizza: 4.69
Popcorn: 0.34
total: 8.02
```

In this part, you decide to remove your cheapest coupon and maximize savings. I feel like I should be clipping coupons out of the Sunday paper or something.

app/simulator.php

```
13    $priceAdjuster->removeAdjustment($coupon1);
14    unset($coupon1);
15    price('removing coupon #1, now 30% benefit back', $product1, $product2, $product3);
```

```
--- removing coupon #1, now 30% benefit back ---
Block Cheese: 2.79
Frozen Pizza: 3.28
Popcorn: 0.24
total: 6.31
```

Lastly, you show that you can edit a benefit and the product prices are automatically changed via the price adjuster mediator.

app/simulator.php

```
13    $benefit1->modifyDiscount(45);
14    price('customer gets 45% discount now!', $product1, $product2, $product3);
```

```
--- customer gets 45% discount now! ---
Block Cheese: 2.19
Frozen Pizza: 2.58
Popcorn: 0.19
total: 4.96
```

That about wraps up this example. I leave you with a few afterthoughts on this pattern below.

Don't Mess with My Constructor, Man!

If you don't like how the mediator pattern junks up your constructors, note that you can change that. You could use a nullable object or even a simple singleton.

app/Product.php

```
public function construct($name, $price, AbstractPriceAdjuster $priceAdjuster = null)
{
        $this->name = $name;
        $this->price = $this->modifiedPrice = $price;
        parent:: construct($priceAdjuster ?: PriceAdjuster::instance());
}
```

And there you have it. No more having to pass in the price adjuster. If you don't pass anything in, it uses a static instance of the price adjuster, a simple singleton. When unit testing, make sure you don't use this singleton, though, by passing your own mock price adjuster in.

Mediator Is Not For Me

You may have noticed that the mediator can quickly become overwhelming. I personally don't like the approach I took for this example. It is an example of trying to make a pattern "fit." You could have avoided the mediator pattern by merely making two calls when updating a product's price: one to update the price and the second to recalculate. Allow me to demonstrate.

```
$product = new Product("name", 3.45);
$product->modifyPrice(2.34);
$priceAdjuster->updatePrice();
```

Now instead of the product calling the mediator, you call it yourself. I like this level of control better myself. Currently, the mediator is coupled to all the colleagues and vice-versa. It seems too complex for what it really is. Hopefully you've learned a bit about the mediator pattern (and enough to know when to stay away from it). Let's talk about what isn't a mediator pattern.

Not a Mediator Pattern

Let me take a moment and point out that managers and controllers are not the same as the mediator pattern. A manager or controller does initialize subordinate classes. Often times those subordinates never directly communicate with each other. Is that not a mediator? No, for several reasons. Firstly, those subordinate classes generally have no way to communicate back to the manager. The communication is one-way. The manager tells the subordinate what to do and waits for a direct response. If something later happens with the subordinate, the manager will remain blissfully unaware because the subordinate has no way to get back in touch with the manager. The second reason is that subordinates are likely not colleagues. They have very little (if anything) to do with each other. The subordinates are likely **not** coupled with each other.

There is the *hexagonal pattern* that can be used with controllers, directors, and manager objects. One might be inclined to think that the hexagonal pattern is much like the mediator pattern. It is structured similarly. The basic idea of the hexagonal pattern is to pass the controller object to the subordinate class. The subordinate can then call methods back on the controller object that was passed in. This sort of resembles the mediator pattern but it is not quite the same. Mediators handle communication across multiple colleagues. The hexagonal pattern only deals with communicating directly between two classes: the Controller and the Service.

In case you're wondering what the hexagonal pattern might look like, here is some example code. You define an interface for the controller to use.

```
interface Created
{
        public function created($obj);
        public function notCreated($errors);
}
```

The controller implements the Created interface. It has to in order to be used by the UserCreator service class that you will soon see. In the following code, the controller is no longer is responsible for actually validating and creating a new user. His job is to act merely as a transport/routing layer and delegating tasks to the subordinate UserCreator class.

```
class UserController extends Controller implements Created
{
        public function store(Request $request)
        {
            $userCreator = new UserCreator($this);
            return $userCreator->create($request->input('email'), $request->input('password'));
        }

        public function created($user)
        {
```

167

```
        auth()->login($user);
        return redirect('/');
    }

    public function notCreated($errors)
    {
        return redirect('users/create')->withErrors($errors)->withInpt();
    }
}
```

Next, you need to define your UserCreator service class. It will handle the job of creating a user. The UserCreator tells the manager if it was created or notCreated by directly calling the manager's methods. Using this approach, notice that your controller is completely logic-less. It's so simple that it doesn't even really need to be tested. You could still unit test the controller if you wanted to but you'd need to refactor so that you could inject a mock UserCreator. Testing your UserCreator is easier since you don't have to deal with facades, HTTP requests, and redirects.

```
class UserCreator
{
    public function construct(Created $manager)
    {
        $this->manager = $manager;
    }

    public function create($email, $password)
    {
        $validator = Validator::make(...);

        if ($validator->fails()) {
            return $this->manager->notCreated($errors);
        }

        $user = new User;
        $user->email = $email;
        $user->password = bcrypt($password);
        $user->save();

        // do other user creation stuff here

        return $this->manager->created($user);
    }
}
```

Another benefit of the hexagonal pattern is that you can reuse your UserCreator class with a different class, like creating users with a console command. The downside of this pattern is that there are now two places you need to check in order to create users: the UserController and the UserCreator. It makes your code a little more complex but offers the flexibility of separating the transport layer and business logic layer.

I could write an entire chapter about the hexagonal pattern but I've covered it briefly here, mainly to illustrate a point. The point is that your UserCreator can communicate back to his manager, which is a similar structure to the mediator pattern. The intent of the hexagonal pattern is to separate transport and business layers. The intent is **not** to decouple colleague objects. My final point is that you should remember that intent is very important when discussing patterns. Especially when you compare differences between patterns.

Conclusion

A mediator pattern is used to handle communication between colleague objects. This promotes loose coupling between classes that could otherwise be tightly coupled. One of the biggest downsides that I've seen while researching this pattern is the creation of god objects. We've all created god objects before. Given enough time, these objects fill your heart with remorse and regret. A buddy and I had a term for this kind of behavior. We called it **the previous asshole**.

The previous asshole is the guy who writes a bunch of code and then leaves. Now you're stuck with a ton of bizarre and strange code that you have to figure out. Sometimes you are even your own previous asshole. You come crawling back to code written months ago, only because the client complained about some bizarre bug. Bizarre code tends to yield bizarre bugs. And mediators tend to yield previous assholes, especially as the number of colleagues increases.

Another downside to this pattern is that when the mediator pattern doesn't fit, you end up creating more complex code than needed. The mediator is a hard pattern to fit into Laravel. A better fit for this pattern might be found in front-end JavaScript. Events are commonly used to propagate changes throughout code, so perhaps it is does better in JavaScript land. My two cents: if you find yourself wanting loose coupling between many objects, give the mediator a once over. Otherwise, leave it be.

Next up, let's take a moment to talk about the memento pattern.

CHAPTER 21

■ ■ ■

Memento

```
$> git checkout memento
```

Intent

Without violating encapsulation, capture and externalize an object's internal state so that the object can be restored to this state later.[1]

Applications

Have you ever seen that movie called Memento[2]? The story follows an investigator who can no longer make new memories. He follows clues in order to find a second attacker on his murdered wife. It's not one of Christopher Nolan's best movies but it is still worth watching. This chapter has nothing to do with that. I'm not even sure how to relate the movie with the memento pattern. I do love a good Nolan film, though.

The reason you use the memento pattern is to save the internal state of an object. This pattern is also known as the *undo* pattern. You create snapshots of an object. And you can revert back to a previous state at any time.

Taking snapshots of objects might sound easy. You look at an object and copy values, right? Well, it's not quite that simple. Look at the object below and ask yourself, how do you save the internal variables state of MyObject?

app/MyObject.php

```php
namespace App;

class MyObject
{
    private $thing;
    public $anotherThing;
}
```

You can access $anotherThing because it is public. Saving the value of $thing is difficult because it is a private variable. You could create a public method called getThing() to get around this. At this point, you are creating methods for the sake of saving private values. This is exposing the inner workings of the class and breaking encapsulation.

---

[1]*Design Patterns: Elements of Reusable Object-Oriented Software*, p. 315
[2]http://en.wikipedia.org/wiki/Memento_%28film%29

© Kelt Dockins 2017
K. Dockins, *Design Patterns in PHP and Laravel*, DOI 10.1007/978-1-4842-2451-9_21

Why does this *break* encapsulation? Imagine you have a box. When you push a button on the box, it spits

out a chocolate cake. That is encapsulation. Now imagine there are a hundred buttons on the cake maker box. You can make different size cakes and different flavors. A machine with over hundred buttons sounds really complicated. It is a pain to create one. It is a pain to maintain it. It is also a pain to use. I mean, if I just want chocolate cakes, I shouldn't have to mess with 99 buttons. In software design, you strive to create **a hundred different cake machines with just one button rather than one cake machine with a hundred buttons**.

You aren't building cake machines. You are building objects. The same principles apply, though. When you design your objects, you should strive to make them as easy to use as possible. In order to do that, your class should have the least amount of responsibility possible. The more public methods you create for your classes, the more responsibilities you add. This is why you use the memento pattern rather than exposing private variables.

A great way to keep from exposing private variables **yet** saving them for later use is to use the memento pattern. So let's learn how.

Abstract Structure

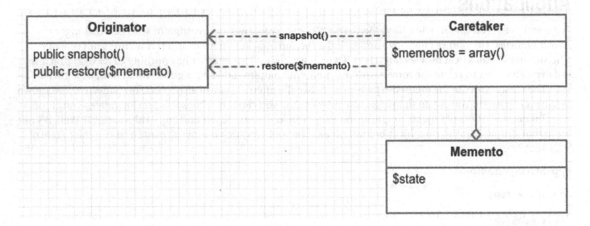

Figure 21-1. Abstract structure

- Originator is the class that has the public, protected, and private variables you want to save. When you call the snapshot method on Originator, it will create a new Memento object. The restore method allows you to set private and protected variables inside this class. See Figure 21-1.

- Caretaker handles the snapshots. The Originator does not need the extra responsibility of holding on to its own snapshots. It is up to the caretaker to determine how you restore snapshots later. This could be done by an undo method. It could be done by picking a numerical index from the $mementos array. It could be totally random. It is up to the caretaker to decide how to restore mementos back into the Originator.

- Memento is the plain old PHP object (POPO) that stores the variables you saved from your Originator. It is important that you do not change these variables. This violates the memento pattern in a way. Snapshots should be seen as immutable. Once you start tampering with a Memento object, you are creating a tight coupling between the Memento and the Originator. At that point, it is no longer a memento. It becomes something else entirely different.

 This pattern has no abstract interfaces. Weird, huh? Singleton and facade are the only other patterns that don't have abstract interfaces. I will actually use an interface in the example below because I find interfaces nice to work with. I mention this to illustrate a point. You don't **always** have to use interfaces *just* to use a pattern. Regardless of whether or not you are using an interface, you may still be using a design pattern. I know at this point I probably sound like a broken record, but I'll say it again: **it's the intent, not code structure, that really determines a design pattern**.

Example

Your goal is to take snapshots of your Eloquent models. A snapshot should hold all the required information to restore a model back to its original state. This means if you change attributes, table name, and other properties on the model, you can always revert back to a previous snapshot.

In this example, you will learn more about the internals of Eloquent. You will also diverge from the UML slightly and make use of traits to implement your memento pattern. The traits are not necessary but I find in this case it adds a little bit of syntax sugar to the code as a whole.

Using your snapshots trait, you will make snapshots of your Eloquent models. There are numerous benefits from doing this. One is that at any time you can create a snapshot of a model and then revert it back to some original state. Perhaps you are changing the e-mail address of a person object, and you save it in the database. If things go wrong, maybe you want to restore the person object as it was before. After updating a person's information, you need to update the information on some remote service, like Stripe, CRM, or a search index. You will create a snapshot of your person. if something goes wrong with updating the remote service, you will restore your person from the snapshot.

But *wouldn't database transactions or an audit history table be more appropriate?* Yes, this is true. In fact, database transactions are a real-life example of the memento pattern. **Furthermore,** there is nothing keeping you from implementing an audit history as part of your memento pattern. You won't do it for this example, but you could easily add in audits later when snapshots are taken.

Example Structure

Figure 22-2 shows the structure.

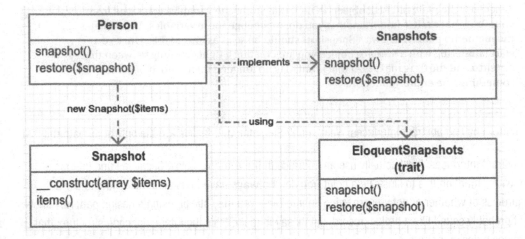

Figure 21-2. Example structure

Implementation

Let's take a look at your snapshot object. This takes the place of the memento object. You construct the snapshot with an array of key/value pairs. Notice that you cannot alter your items after the snapshot is created. This is done on purpose to keep the caretaker from breaking encapsulation.

app/Snapshot.php

```php
namespace App;

class Snapshot
{
    protected $items;

    public function __construct(array $items)
    {
        $this->items = $items;
    }

    public function items()
    {
        return $this->items;
    }
}
```

Instead of passing in a generic array called $items you could have been explicit and listed out the actual properties you are snapshotting. You are certainly welcome to do that as well. This generic snapshot class is abstract enough to handle many different types of Originators. The Originator is the only one who should be consuming the snapshot. Your snapshot class has only one responsibility. It acts as a bucket of key/value pairs. The more the snapshot class knows about the Originator, the more likely you jeopardize encapsulation of the Originator.

The snapshot class above knows nothing about the Originator. There is a drawback to not being explicit about the properties of the Originator. The Originator must be extra careful when creating the snapshot. When the Originator forgets to set a key, there is no compilation error like there would be if you instead had to explicitly provide all the Originator's properties to the snapshot constructor. Being explicit often prevent bugs later. In this case, you make an exception and choose the implicit path.

Next, look at your Originator object.

app/Person.php

```
namespace App;

class Person extends Model implements Snapshots
{
        use EloquentSnapshots;
}
```

You use a trait here to implement your Snapshots interface. This practice is becoming more and more common in Laravel. The Snapshots interface merely requires you to implement two methods.

app/Snapshots.php

```
namespace App;

interface Snapshots
{
        public function snapshot();
        public function restore(Snapshot $snapshot);
}
```

You use the trait to mix in this functionality. You could write the methods directly inside your Person class. There are two reasons why you choose to do a trait instead. One is for reusability. This trait is generic enough that it can be reused by other Eloquent models. The second reason is to keep from having to inherit from another base class besides Eloquent.

app/EloquentSnapshots.php

```
namespace App;

trait EloquentSnapshots
{
        public function snapshot()
        {
                $items = [];

                $keys = [
                        'connection', 'table', 'primaryKey',
                        'perPage', 'incrementing', 'timestamps',
                        'attributes', 'original', 'relations',
                        'hidden', 'visible', 'appends',
                        'fillable', 'guarded', 'dates',
                        'touches', 'observables', 'with',
                        'morphClass', 'exists',
                ];

                foreach ($keys as $key) {
                        $items[$key] = $this->$key;
                }
                return new Snapshot($items);
        }
}
```

You loop through all the keys and add them into a key/value pair array called $items. The items are then used to create a new snapshot object. Later the snapshot object will be used to loop back through the items you added and assign them back into your Eloquent class.

app/EloquentSnapshots.php

```php
public function restore(Snapshot $snapshot)
{
        foreach ($snapshot->items() as $key => $value) {
                $this->$key = $value;
        }
}
```

Now all that is left is the caretaker. The caretaker manages the snapshots created from the Originator. You aren't going to make that class in your example; instead the simulator will manage the snapshots for you. In a way, the simulator assumes the role of the caretaker.

app/simulator.php

```php
9   $person = new \App\Person;
10  $person->name = "Kelt";
11  $snapshot1 = $person->snapshot();
12
13  $person->setTable('persons');
14  $person->name = "test name";
15  $person->email = "testing@test.com";
16  $snapshot2 = $person->snapshot();
```

Notice you created two snapshots. The first snapshot only has "Kelt" in the name. The second snapshot changed the person's name and e-mail address. It also set the table name. Let's examine the output of the follow statements:

app/simulator.php

```php
18  print personInfo("this is how person looks now", $person);
```

console output

```
this is how person looks now
name: test name, table: persons, email: testing@test.com
```

app/simulator.php

```php
20  $person->restore($snapshot1);
21  print personInfo("restoring snapshot 1", $person);
```

console output

```
restoring snapshot 1
name: Kelt, table: people, email:
```

app/simulator.php

```php
23  $person->restore($snapshot2);
24  print personInfo("restoring snapshot 2", $person);
```

console output

```
restoring snapshot 2
name: test name, table: persons, email: testing@test.com
```

See how you were able to revert your object to a previous snapshot? You print off the table name, person name, and e-mail as evidence that the snapshots are working. The first and third printed statements are the same, as expected. Of course you've peeked behind the curtain, so you know how the magic is working behind the scenes. This is still pretty cool, though. You get to create snapshots of your Eloquent model and at any time you can undo changes just by restoring the snapshot.

Alternatives to Memento

Whenever I encounter a problem, I always try to remember to check how other people solved the problem. This can often save me time. That being said, let's propose a couple of alternatives to using the memento pattern with Eloquent.

1. Using Eloquent methods

2. Object serialization

Using Eloquent Methods

Not surprisingly, Eloquent already has a method called syncOriginal. Taylor uses this array to keep track of what has changed in your Eloquent model since you last saved it. There are methods called isDirty and getDirty that check for changes in your Eloquent model. They compare the contents of the $original array with the $attributes array.

vendor/laravel/framework/src/Illuminate/Database/Eloquent/Model.php

```
3217    public function getDirty()
3218    {
3219            $dirty = [];
3220
3221            foreach ($this->attributes as $key => $value) {
3222                if (! array_key_exists($key, $this->original)) {
3223                    $dirty[$key] = $value;
3224                } elseif ($value !== $this->original[$key] &&
3225                            ! $this->originalIsNumericallyEquivalent($key)) {
3226                    $dirty[$key] = $value;
3227                }
3228            }
3229    }
```

This method allows you to see the dirty fields. After an Eloquent model is finished saving, you sync the original array. This means that nothing should be considered dirty once you have saved the model.

vendor/laravel/framework/src/Illuminate/Database/Eloquent/Model.php

```
1502    protected function finishSave(array $options)
1503    {
1504            $this->fireModelEvent('saved', false);
1505
1506            $this->syncOriginal();
1507
1508            if (Arr::get($options, 'touch', true)) {
1509                $this->touchOwners();
1510            }
1511    }
```

After you finish saving a model, the $attributes array is copied to $original by the syncOriginal method.

vendor/laravel/framework/src/Illuminate/Database/Eloquent/Model.php

```
3154    public function syncOriginal()
3155    {
3156            $this->original = $this->attributes;
3157
3158            return $this;
3159    }
```

Why am I covering all of this? It's good for you to know how Eloquent handles certain things. Seeing how Taylor handles this problem can give you ideas for your own problems. By looking under the hood, you ensure that Taylor isn't doing snapshots or the memento pattern. You did find that he is keeping track of attributes in an array. This is handy. This means that if you only want a snapshot of your attributes, Taylor has you covered. You can use getAttributes().

app/test1.php

```
$person1 = new \App\Person;
$person1->name = 'Kelt';
$snapshot1 = $person1->getAttributes();

$person2 = new Person($snapshot1);
print personInfo('New person from attributes of person1', $person2);
```

    console output

```
New person from attributes of person1
name: Kelt, table: people, email:
```

This code requires no special coding on your part. It's all baked into Eloquent already. If all you need to do is restore attributes, then you don't need the memento pattern.

Object Serialization

Another option you can choose is object serialization. Instead of creating the memento pattern, you serialize an object, thus saving it as a string. The string can be stored for later use. When you need to restore, you unserialize the string back into an object. It's a nice way to create snapshots.

app/test2.php

```php
$person = new \App\Person;
$person->setTable('persons');
$person->email = 'testing@test.com';
$snapshot1 = serialize($person);

$person->setTable('crm_people');
$person->email = "some-new@email.com";
print personInfo('examining person object', $person);

$person = unserialize($snapshot1);
print personInfo('restoring snapshot 1', $person);
```

    console output

```
examining person object
name: , table: crm_people, email: some-new@email.com
restoring snapshot 1
name: , table: persons, email: testing@test.com
```

Why would you not just serialize objects? Why even use the memento pattern at all? The memento pattern offers a few advantages over serialization. The first advantage the memento pattern offers is flexibility and control. If you simply serialize your object, you don't get the option of cherry picking which fields you might want to save. What if you only want to save a couple of protected properties? The memento pattern allows you to choose only those fields you want to save.

Most objects can be serialized. Objects that contain a resource, such as a database connection or file stream, can have issues. There are some cases where serialization fails to work. This is the second benefit of the memento pattern. You don't have to deal with sleep and wakeup or the Serializable[3] interface when you use the memento pattern. You shouldn't be afraid to deal with serialization, though. Object serialization is pretty cool. The below test shows that Eloquent still seems to handle serialization for you, even when you have made a connection to the database. Check it out.

app/test3.php

```php
$person = new \App\Person;
$person->email = 'testing@test.com';
$person->save();

$snapshot1 = serialize($person);
$person->email = "something@else.com";
$person = unserialize($snapshot1);
```

---

[3]http://php.net/manual/en/class.serializable.php

```
print $person->isDirty() === false ? '' : 'isDirty' . PHP_EOL;
print personInfo('unserialized person', $person);
```

    console output

```
unserialized person
name: , table: people, email: testing@test.com
```

 You have to run migrations in order for the above code to work. You also need the SQLite PHP PDO driver installed on your machine.

Serialization can take you a long way. Even with the advantages of the memento pattern, serialization is still a really cool option.

Conclusion

The memento pattern is used to avoid violating encapsulation while still capturing internal variables of an originator class. There are some downsides to the memento pattern. The cost of creating memento objects can be memory intensive when the originator object has a lot of data to store. The second downside of this pattern is that you are adding more responsibilities to the originator object.

You've learned alternatives to the memento pattern, too. All in all, this pattern can likely be replaced by serialization alternative, provided you don't need any extra flexibility when creating your snapshots.

CHAPTER 22

Observer

```
$> git checkout observer
```

Intent

Define a one-to-many dependency between objects so that when one object changes state, all its dependents are notified and updated automatically.[1]

Applications

The observer pattern is used when you want objects to react to specific events on a subject object. When the subject changes, it notifies observers. This is one of the most popular patterns I will cover. In fact, PHP already has built-in interfaces for the observer pattern: SplSubject[2] and SplObserver[3].

Abstract Structure

- SplSubject is an abstract class or interface. When using an abstract class, you might place an array here to keep up with the attached observers. The SplSubject contains three methods. The attach method adds observers to this subject. The detach method takes away observers. The notify method usually contains a loop that iterates over all the attached observers and calls their update method.

- SplObserver is an abstract class or interface. The SplObserver interface contains one method called update which is triggered by the SplSubject whenever the subject updates.

- RealSubject is an implementation of the SplSubject. It will contain the storage object (array/collection/etc.) needed to hang on the attached observers. Some implementations actually create an abstract class in place of SplSubject and place the storage object in the abstract class instead. Since SplSubject is an interface, you can't do this. There is nothing stopping you from creating your own abstract class instead of using an interface, though.

---

[1] *Design Patterns: Elements of Reusable Object-Oriented Software*, p. 326
[2] http://php.net/manual/en/class.splsubject.php
[3] http://php.net/manual/en/class.splobserver.php

© Kelt Dockins 2017
K. Dockins, *Design Patterns in PHP and Laravel*, DOI 10.1007/978-1-4842-2451-9_22

- RealObserver is an implementation of the SplObserver interface. It's update method will be passed an instance of SplSubject. This class handles the specific logic needed to execute whenever the subject is updated.

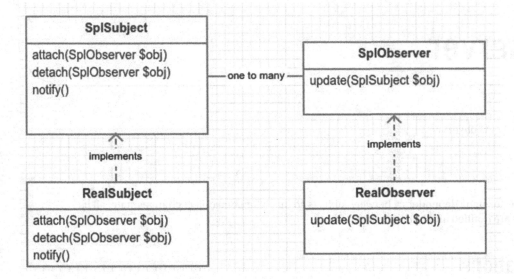

Figure 22-1. *Abstract structure*

Example

In this example, you are going to show a rather generic version of the observer pattern using PHP's built-in SplObserver and SplSubject. After getting that out of the way, you will move onto a more intricate situation where Taylor cuts the cheese and those observing nearby smell it. Finally, you will wrap up the chapter using observers on Eloquent models. You will also explore some of the internals of Laravel's Eloquent models and how it uses events to handle attached observers.

Example Structure

Figure 22-2 shows the structure.

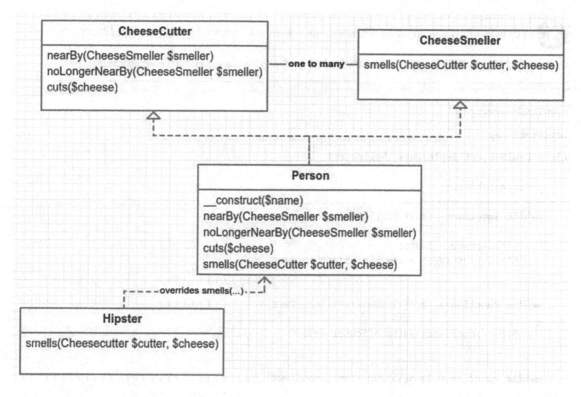

Figure 22-2. Example structure

Implementation

Generic Observers with SPL

You only need to create two classes since you are using the generic SPL interfaces.

app/RealObserver.php

```php
namespace App;

class RealObserver implements \SplObserver
{
    public function __construct($name)
    {
        $this->name = $name;
    }

    public function update(\SplSubject $subject)
    {
        print "{$this->name} was notified by {$subject->name}" . PHP_EOL;
    }
}
```

In case you're wondering what SPL stands for, it is an abbreviation for *Standard Php Library*. There are many neat things in the SPL. You can see them at http://php.net/manual/en/book.spl.php.

app/RealSubject.php

namespace App;

```php
class RealSubject implements \SplSubject
{
    private $observers;

    public function __construct($name)
    {
        $this->name = $name;
        $this->observers = new \SplObjectStorage;
    }

    public function attach(\SplObserver $observer)
    {
        $this->observers->attach($observer);
    }

    public function detach(\SplObserver $observer)
    {
        $this->observers->detach($observer);
    }

    public function notify()
    {
        foreach ($this->observers as $observer) {
            $observer->update($this);
        }
    }
}
```

Take note of the SplObjectStorage object. Notice that when you want to detach an observer, you merely call detach on the SplObjectStorage object. What if you had just used arrays here? You would have to loop through the observers array and find the observer to remove. Then you would have to unset it. The SplObjectStorage is a neat helper class. I know I've already said this, but I'll say it again. I recommend you check out more standard PHP libraries[4].

These two classes, RealSubject and RealObserver, are about as generic as it gets. It's difficult to look at these two classes and derive any business meaning behind them. This is one of the downsides of using SplSubject and SplObserver. You are stuck with the generic methods. You also cannot type hint anything other than SplSubject to the update method. It is almost not worth using them. The SplSubject and SplObserver are good for guidance, I suppose. Nevertheless, let's run your simulation and see some test output.

---

[4]http://php.net/manual/en/book.spl.php

app/simulator.php

```
$subject1 = new \App\RealSubject('subject1');
$observer1 = new \App\RealObserver('observer1');
$observer2 = new \App\RealObserver('observer2');
$observer3 = new \App\RealObserver('observer3');

$subject1->attach($observer1);
$subject1->attach($observer2);
$subject1->attach($observer3);

$subject1->notify();
```

console output

```
> php app/simulator.php
observer1 was notified by subject1
observer2 was notified by subject1
observer3 was notified by subject1
```

And there you have it. As one last note, I want to point out here that you may not always want your notify method to be public. You may only want observers to be notified when internal processes happen. Unfortunately, you can't change that here, again, due to the restrictions of using the generic SPL interfaces. Let's get a little more custom in the next section.

Taylor Cuts the Cheese

You all know people are complex. They can observe **and** be observed. Another way of putting that: people are both **subjects** and **observers**. In the next example, you will tell a story. The story goes like this.

It was a quiet day. Taylor was hanging out with his Laravel groupies on #laravel irc. Suddenly, Taylor cut the cheese. No one really noticed. Except for Jeffery, Machuga, Dayle. Oh, Adam, Matt and Graham Campbell. These guys happened to be paying attention and nearby. Taylor doesn't like to share his Monterrey Jack cheese. He decided to leave the channel and enjoy his cheese alone. Translated into code, it looks like this:

app/cheese.php

```
$taylor = new \App\Person("Taylor");
$dayle = new \App\Person("Dayle");
$jeffery = new \App\Person("Jeffery");
$machuga = new \App\Hipster("Machuga");
$campbell = new \App\Person('Graham');

$taylor->nearBy($dayle, $jeffery, $machuga, $campbell);
$taylor->cuts('cheedar');
$taylor->says('oops...');

$taylor->noLongerNearBy($dayle, $jeffery, $machuga);
$taylor->cuts('monterey jack');
$taylor->says('This monterey jack cheese is all mine! muhahaha!');
```

For this code, you expect output like this:

console output

```
> php app/cheese.php
--- Taylor cuts cheedar ---
Dayle says:        "i smell cheedar"
Jeffery says:      "i smell cheedar"
Machuga says:      "i smell cheedarz, that you Taylor?"
Graham says:       "i smell cheedar"
Taylor says:       "oops..."
--- Taylor cuts monterey jack ---
Taylor says:       "This monterey jack cheese is all mine! muhahaha!"
```

The above code doesn't work yet, though. You still have to create the underlying classes. Let's start with your basic interfaces: the cheese smeller and cheese cutter.

app/CheeseSmeller.php

```php
namespace App;

interface CheeseSmeller
{
        public function smells(CheeseCutter $cutter, $cheese);
}
```

app/CheeseCutter.php

```php
namespace App;

interface CheeseCutter
{
        public function nearBy(CheeseSmeller $smeller);
        public function noLongerNearBy(CheeseSmeller $smeller);
        public function cuts($cheese);
}
```

A person has a name in your story. You will need to provide the name in the constructor. A person can also speak, so you need a method for that too.

app/Person.php

```php
class Person implements CheeseSmeller, CheeseCutter
{
        public function __construct($name)
        {
                $this->name = $name;
                $this->nearBy = new \SplObjectStorage;
        }

        public function says($phrase)
        {
                print "{$this->name} says: \t\"" . $phrase . "\"" . PHP_EOL;
        }
```

You need to implement nearBy. This method keeps track of nearby smellers.

app/Person.php

```
16    public function nearBy(CheeseSmeller $smeller)
17    {
18            $smellers = func_get_args();
19
20            foreach ($smellers as $smeller) {
21
22                    $this->nearBy->attach($smeller);
23            }
24    }
```

Next, you implement noLongerNearBy. This removes any smellers that might have been nearby this person.

app/Person.php

```
26    public function noLongerNearBy(CheeseSmeller $smeller)
27    {
28            $smellers = func_get_args();
29
30            foreach ($smellers as $smeller) {
31
32                    $this->nearBy->detach($smeller);
33            }
34    }
```

When a person cuts the cheese, anyone nearby will smell it.

app/Person.php

```
36    public function cuts($cheese)
37    {
38            print "--- {$this->name} cuts {$cheese} ---" . PHP_EOL;
39
40            foreach ($this->nearBy as $nearBy) {
41
42                    $nearBy->smells($this, $cheese);
43            }
44    }
```

Lastly, as part of your CheeseSmeller interface, you need to implement smells. This method is called whenever a person was nearby another person that cut the cheese.

app/Person.php

```
46    public function smells(CheeseCutter $cutter, $cheese)
47    {
48            $this->says("i smell {$cheese}");
49    }
```

And there you have it. Unlike the generic SPL example you covered earlier, this code **reeks** of business logic. You can look at these method names and discover what is happening. Both the SPL example and this cheese cutting example use the observer pattern. Next, you will examine the observer pattern embedded deep inside all of your Eloquent models.

Eloquent Observers: Out-of-the-Box Observers

All Eloquent models have the observer pattern baked in. For the next example, you will create a Car model. A car has a some attributes: manufacturer, vin, description, and year. Feel free to check out the seeder[5] and migration[6]. You may not need to run seeds and migration since I also committed the database.sqlite database to the GitHub repository.

app/Car.php

```
namespace App;

use Illuminate\Database\Eloquent\Model;

class Car extends Model
{
}
```

Now you have an Eloquent model. How do you set observers on this model? You use the observe method.

app/test1.php

```
\App\Car::observe(new Observers\ObserveEverything);
```

Below I have made a generic observer called ObserverEverything, which contains all of the *out-of-the-box* methods you can observe on an Eloquent model. Each method simply prints a statement so that you can get an idea of when it is being invoked. Let's take a look at this list of methods.

app/Observers/ObserveEverything.php

```
namespace App\Observers;

class ObserveEverything
{
        public function creating($model)
        {
                print "creating model" . PHP_EOL;
        }

        public function created($model)
        {
                print "created model" . PHP_EOL;
        }

        public function updating($model)
        {
                print "updating model" . PHP_EOL;
        }
```

---

[5]https://github.com/kdocki/larasign/blob/observer/database/seeds/DatabaseSeeder.php
[6]https://github.com/kdocki/larasign/blob/observer/database/migrations/2015_03_10_222303_create_cars_table.php

```php
    public function updated($model)
    {
            print "updated model" . PHP_EOL;
    }

    public function saving($model)
    {
            print "saving model" . PHP_EOL;

    }
    public function saved($model)
    {
            print "saved model" . PHP_EOL;
    }

    public function deleting($model)
    {
            print "deleting model" . PHP_EOL;
    }

    public function deleted($model)
    {
            print "deleted model" . PHP_EOL;
    }

    public function restoring($model)
    {
            print "restoring model" . PHP_EOL;
    }

    public function restored($model)
    {
            print "restored model" . PHP_EOL;
    }
}
```

You can guess from each method name and figure out when it will be called. However, I've listed each here with further insight.

- creating is called before a model is first created in database. You can trigger this is by calling save on a freshly constructed model or by using create statically. Note that this method is not triggered when a new model is constructed or retrieved from database. If the method returns false, the model will not be created.

- created is called after the model has been created in the database.

- updating is called before existing models are saved in the database. If the method returns false, the model is not updated.

- updated is called after existing models are saved in the database.

- saving is called before a model is created or updated in the database. If the method returns false, the model is not saved.

- saved is called after a model is created or updated in the database.

- deleting is called before a model is deleted from the database. If method returns false, the model is not deleted.

- deleted is called after a model is deleted from the database.

- restoring is called before a model is restored in the database. A restore is only available for models that use Laravel's soft deletes. This removes the date from this record's deleted_at column in the database. If the method returns false, the model is not restored.

- restored is called after a model is restored in the database.

The next step is to attach this observer to your Car model.

app/test1.php

```
7   Car::observe(new Observers\ObserveEverything);
```

You will trigger events by making changes to the Car model. The following further shows which methods inside the ObserveEverything observer are invoked.

app/test1.php

```
10  $car1 = Car::find(1);
11  $car1->vin = str_random()(32);
12  print "\nSaving car #1 to database\n";
13  $car1->save();

Saving car #1 to database
saving model
updating model
updated model
saved model
```

app/test1.php

```
17  $car2 = new Car;
18  $car2->description = "cool car description";
19  $car2->vin = str_random(32);
20  $car2->manufacturer = 'Honda';
21  $car2->year = '2012';
22  print "\nCreating new car\n";
23  $car2->save();

Creating new car
saving model
creating model
created model
saved model
```

app/test1.php

```
26  print "\nDeleting that new car you just made\n";
27  $car2->delete();
```

```
Deleting that new car you just made
deleting model
deleted model
```

app/test1.php

```
30    print "\nRestoring that car you just deleted\n";
31    $car2->restore();
```

```
Restoring that car you just deleted
restoring model
saving model
updating model
updated model
saved model
restored model
```

Preventing Updates with Observers

You might have noticed a reoccurring pattern with these *out-of-the-box* observer events. Each one offers an observer the ability to *hook* into **before** and **after** events on the Eloquent model. One feature provided is that if you return false on any **before** type of event then further execution stops. This means you can **prevent** an Eloquent model from saving, creating, updating, deleting, or restoring using observers. Let's see an example.

Say all VIN numbers for a car must contain the letter *h*. Using an observer, you will prevent updates to the database when a VIN does not contain the letter *h*.

app/test1.php

```
7     Car::observe(new Observers\VinObserver);
8     $car1 = Car::find(1);
9
10    // attempt #1 with no h
11    $car1->vin = "asdfasdfasdf";
12    $car1->save() && print "attempt #1 saved\n";
13
14    // attempt #2 contains h
15    $car1->vin = "hasdfasdfasdf";
16    $car1->save() && print "attempt #2 saved\n";
```

```
model vin does not contain letter 'h', canceling update...
attempt #2 saved
```

The first attempt fails to update. Only the second attempt saves to the database. Here is the VinObserver that enforces the *h* rule.

app/Observers/VinObserver.php

namespace App\Observers;

class VinObserver
```
{
        public function updating($model)
        {
                $original = $model->getOriginal('vin');
```

```
            if ($model->vin === $original) {
                    return true;    // ignore unchanged vin
            }

            if (! str_contains($model->vin, 'h')) {

                    print "model vin does not contain letter 'h', canceling updating vi \n";

                    return false;
            }
        }

}
```

You ignore any models that have not changed their VIN number. The VINs that have changed without the letter *h* return false. This prevents updates from occurring. So how does Laravel handle this for you under the hood? Let's take a peek for updates.

vendor/laravel/framework/src/Illuminate/Database/Eloquent/Model.php

```
1520    protected function performUpdate(Builder $query, array $options = [])
1521    {
1522        if ($this->fireModelEvent('updating') === false) {
1523            return false;
1524        }
1525
1526        if ($this->timestamps && Arr::get($options, 'touch', true)) {
1527            $this->updateTimestamps();
1528        }
1529
1530        $dirty = $this->getDirty();
1531
1532        if (count($dirty) > 0) {
1533            $this->setKeysForSaveQuery($query)->update($dirty);
1534            $this->fireModelEvent('updated', false);
1535        }
1536
1537        return true;
```

When you are performing an update, the one thing that happens is a check for dirty fields. If nothing has changed on this model, then you don't even need to update. Next, you can see the fireModelEvent. If it returns a false, then you don't perform the update. Let's go ahead and examine the fireModelEvent method.

vendor/laravel/framework/src/Illuminate/Database/Eloquent/Model.php

```
1651    protected function fireModelEvent($event, $halt = true)
1652    {
1653        if (! isset(static::$dispatcher)) {
1654            return true;
1655        }
1656
1657        // You will append the names of the class to the event to distinguish it from
1658        // other model events that are fired, allowing you to listen on each\model
1659        // event set individually instead of catching event for all the models.
```

```
1660        $event = "eloquent.{$event}: ".static::class;
1661
1662        $method = $halt ? 'until' : 'fire';
1663
1664        return static::$dispatcher->$method($event, $this);
1665    }
```

This method calls either *until* or *fire* on the dispatcher and returns the results. Why don't you see any references to observers on this model? All the observers you attach to a model are placed in the dispatcher. That is why you don't see anything about observers in this fireModelEvent method.

So what is this static dispatcher thing? Eloquent models use a shared dispatcher, specifically the $app['events'] singleton. The events dispatcher is a message bus. It is an instance of Illuminate\Events\ Dispatcher. The events dispatcher is injected into Eloquent models when the application boots up the database service provider.

vendor/laravel/framework/src/Illuminate/Database/DatabaseServiceProvider.php

```
20    public function boot()
21    {
22            Model::setConnectionResolver($this->app['db']);
23
24            Model::setEventDispatcher($this->app['events']);
25    }
```

So you've uncovered how model events are fired. You've seen how to prevent updates to a model. However, you are still missing a piece. You've assumed that all registered observers are placed in the event dispatcher somehow because fireModelEvent is using the dispatcher. You don't know how, though. So let's trace through how an observer gets attached to an Eloquent model and the underlying dispatcher to demystify this cloudy mystery.

vendor/laravel/framework/src/Illuminate/Database/Eloquent/Model.php

```
407    public static function observe($class)
408    {
409            $instance = new static;
410
411            $className = is_string($class) ? $class : get_class($class);
412
413            // When registering a model observer, you ...
414            // ... do moose stuff ... (not really)
415            // ... making it convenient to watch these.
416            foreach ($instance->getObservableEvents() as $event) {
417                if (method_exists($class, $event)) {
418                    static::registerModelEvent($event, $className.'@'.$event, $priority);
419                }
420            }
421    }
```

When you call the observe method on a model, it spins through the possible events and then calls registerModelEvent with the event and class name. The getObservableEvents method returns an array of strings. The strings are events you saw earlier (updating, updated, creating, created, and so on). It also includes any additional observable events you have placed on this class using the $observables array. You will actually attach more observable events on your Cars model in the next example. Using substitution, you can deduce in your current example the method has the following arguments:

```
static::registerModelEvent('updating', 'Observers\VinObserver@updating');
```

So what does registerModelEvent do exactly? Let's check it out.

vendor/laravel/framework/src/Illuminate/Database/Eloquent/Model.php

```
1270   protected static function registerModelEvent($event, $callback)
1271   {
1272           if (isset(static::$dispatcher)) {
1273               $name = static::class;
1274               static::$dispatcher->listen("eloquent.{$event}: {$name}", $callback, $priority);
1275           }
1276   }
```

The shared dispatcher is told to listen for an eloquent.updating: App\Cars event. Whenever that event is fired on the dispatcher, the callback will be triggered. This is how observers are attached to an Eloquent model. Notice that each model doesn't get its own array of observers. The observers are all shared within a single dispatcher. This uses less memory than attaching an array of observers on each instance of the Cars model. It also means that all Car models have the same observers, which is expected. If you wanted to create an observer specifically for one instance of a Car but not another, then you'd need to do something different. I'll leave that one for you to ponder. Next up, now that you understand how observers are attached and triggered in an Eloquent model, let's make your own customer observer event.

Adding a Custom Observer

Out of the box there are no observable events for finding and found. You will create these. These events will be called whenever you attempt to find a specific model by id using Car::find($id). Much like it's **before** counterparts, if finding returns false, then you halt execution, preventing the model from being found.

app/test3.php

```
7    \App\Car::observe(new \App\Observers\LookupObserver);
8
9    $car0 = Car::find(0);
10   $car1 = Car::find(1);
finding id 1!
found model 1
```

There is no car with an id of zero. Your lookup observer will prevent any invalid ids from being fetched. You could introduce other things here too. Perhaps each time you look up a Car, it updates some analytics database table.

app/Observers/LookupObserver.php

```php
namespace App\Observers;

class LookupObserver
{
        public function finding($id)
        {
                if ($id < 1) return false;

                print "finding id {$id}!\n";
        }
        public function found($model)
        {
                print "found model {$model->id}\n";
        }
}
```

There are no finding or found events on Eloquent models. So there is still more work you have to do in order for the above code to work. The remaining work is done within the Car model itself.

app/Car.php

```php
class Car extends Model
{
        use SoftDeletes;

        protected $dates = ['deleted_at'];

        protected $observables = ['finding', 'found'];
```

You are using soft deletes, so that is what the first two lines do. The $observables array allows you to listen for other events. It is used within Eloquent's getObservableEvents method. This method merges custom observer events with the de facto standard events.

vendor/laravel/framework/src/Illuminate/Database/Eloquent/Model.php

```php
1284    public function getObservableEvents()
1285    {
1286            return array_merge(
1287                    [
1288                            'creating', 'created', 'updating', 'updated',
1289                            'deleting', 'deleted', 'saving', 'saved',
1290                            'restoring', 'restored',
1291                    ],
1292                    $this->observables // <-- merge in custom events
1293            );
1294    }
```

Back to your Car model, you are going to override the find method. This method will fire your model events for you.

app/Car.php

```
13    public static function find($id, $columns = ['*'])
14    {
15            $shouldProceed = static::triggerModelEvent('finding', true, $id);
16
17            if ($shouldProceed === false) return null;
18
19            $results = parent::find($id, $columns);
20
21            static::triggerModelEvent('found', $stop = false, $results);
22
23            return $results;
24    }
```

Inside this method is a call to the parent find method. The results are returned. You have wrapped triggerModelEvent around the parent find method, though. This allows you to execute the events properly.

Notice that you can't use fireModelEvent because the find method is static. You don't even have an instance of your model yet (because you haven't found it!). Thus you will need to introduce your own way of triggering model events statically. Note that if you already had an instance of the model, you would use fireModelEvent instead of triggerModelEvent.

app/Car.php

```
26    protected static function triggerModelEvent($event, $halt, $params =
27    null)
28    {
29            if (! isset(static::$dispatcher)) return true;
30
31            $event = "eloquent.{$event}: ".get_called_class();
32
33            $method = $halt ? 'until' : 'fire';
34
35            return static::$dispatcher->$method($event, $params);
36    }
```

You mirror the functionality of the fireModelEvent method. It calls the dispatcher much in the same way as fireModelEvent. However, this is a little more flexible. It allows you to provide custom parameters instead of assuming that you already have an instance of an Eloquent model to work with.

Conclusion

Event-driven architecture[7] is a software architecture pattern that revolves around the state within an application. The observer pattern can be used in this type of software architecture. There are other similar patterns. I will list them here because they all are slightly different.

- The observer pattern attaches observer objects to a subject. When the subject state changes, it notifies observers. The observer pattern seems to be a more popular choice than the mediator pattern. In fact, the observer pattern wins the award for most popular design pattern.

---

[7]http://en.wikipedia.org/wiki/Event-driven_architecture

- . The mediator pattern uses one object to mediate many others. Unlike the observer pattern, the mediator knows much more about its aggregated subordinate objects because it calls specific methods on each subordinate object.

- The command bus pattern is related to the command pattern. This can be event driven, too. When state changes in one object, it can send a command onto the command bus. The command bus will process the command either immediately or queue the job for later.

- The sub/pub pattern (subscribe/publish) uses a messaging bus to communicate state changes. Laravel has a built-in message bus called Event[8]. You can use Event like so:

```
Event::listen('Illuminate\Auth\Events\Login', function($user) {

    $user->last_login = new DateTime;

    $user->save();
});
```

```
$response = Event::fire('Illuminate\Auth\Events\Login', [$user]);
```

The observer is one of the most popular design patterns you'll find in this book. It has drawbacks like all the other patterns, too.

Drawbacks

The first drawback is that observers are decoupled from the subject. The subject keeps an array of observers. The subject knows very little about its observers. It calls them when state changes. While this offers powerful flexibility, this can also be a drawback. The observer has to be attached to the subject in some place. Where you register is arbitrary. It could be in some bootstrap file, a service provider, or even the some custom file you've made. Imagine you have many different observers attached to a subject and these attachments are all spread out into many different files. It becomes troublesome to manage what observers are attached to the subject.

The other drawback is that state changes become more complex. When the state changes on a subject, observers are called. Each observer is unaware of the other. If you have 15 observers attached to a subject, then each observer works unaware of what its 14 siblings are doing. This type of code is hard to optimize. For example, what if all 15 observers save to the database? Thus any time you make one change to the subject, you end up with 16 database changes. If there are problems, this can be hard to debug! You'd have to track down each observer and figure out which one is the culprit.

Drawbacks aside, the observer pattern is still used in many architectures and applications. It is a powerful ally in the Source and offers the flexibility to monitor state changes within a subject. Use it wisely.

---

[8]http://laravel.com/docs/4.2/events

CHAPTER 23

■ ■ ■

State

```
$> git checkout state
$> composer update
```

Intent

Allow an object to alter its behavior when its internal state changes. The object will appear to change its class.[1]

Applications

The state pattern is a *glove pattern*. When it fits right, it fits just right. In other words, you'll know when you need it. You can use state pattern for modeling things that change behavior during the course of its lifetime.

Ever find yourself using some string variable named $type and a giant cluster of switch/case/if/else statements to determine which methods to call? The state pattern will clean up all those nasty conditions. A vending machine, along with many other real-life machines, use a state pattern. You don't see those states externally. The states of a vending machine all happen internally. Externally, you experience different behaviors. For example, what happens if you hit the purchase button on a vending machine without paying? What about after you've paid? The internal states change the behavior of that button. The button never changes to you (the client).

Abstract Structure

- Client is the main class used. Underlying methods use context and states to change behavior during runtime. Clients don't usually interact with state objects directly. In other words, a user never knows about a new SomeState class. It only uses the public methods on this client. The internal state of the client can change without the user ever really knowing. When the client calls event(), this relays onward to the underlying state's handler. You don't have to store state inside of a Context. You can store it directly inside this class. This is especially true if you don't need to store context data between states. Why not put the $state inside the client object? Because you pass the context to every state's handle method. Thus, any state has the ability to transition using the context object. If you did not do this, you would have to expose a setState() publicly on your client. This would mean that you can control states outside of the class, which probably isn't a good idea as it adds extra complexity (and responsibility) to this client class.

---

[1]*Design Patterns: Elements of Reusable Object-Oriented Software*, p. 338

K. Dockins, *Design Patterns in PHP and Laravel*, DOI 10.1007/978-1-4842-2451-9_23

- Context is passed to all states, which allows for communication between the states. The context is passed to the handlers of every state. A context can be as simple as data storage (StdClass) or it can contain helper methods (such as the method shown in this diagram). The method can be called from any state class. Sometimes states are "stateless" and don't need to communicate with other states. In this case, you don't need a context object. Some implementations of the State pattern I've seen online actually combine Context and Client into a single class. The downside of combining the Client and Context is that it exposes your internal guts. This adds additional responsibility to the client class. You will keep them separate and avoid making the context public.

- State is an interface. All concrete states will implement this interface. It defines the different handle methods for a state. The handle methods should be named after the **events** that can occur. I will talk more about this shortly. For now, just know that there is some terminology coming your way.

  - States: Some state class

  - Events: Available methods on state class

  - Transitions: When a state and an event causes a state change

- ConcreteState1/ConcreteState2 each represent different states. The methods inside provide instruction to the context object. In other words, what should the context object do for **this** state and event? These classes can also change states using the context object's setState method. Whenever you change state, that is known as a *transition*.

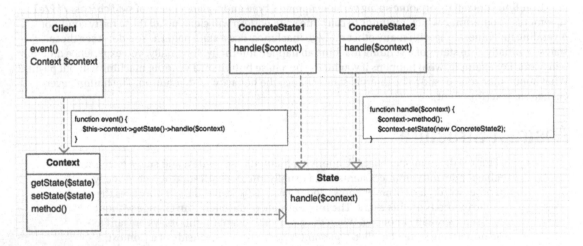

Figure 23-1. Abstract structure

Example

Let's model a vending machine. You can push buttons on a vending machine. Depending on its internal state, it will do different things. *Same button, different response.* You can model a vending machine using a drawing of a finite state machine. See Figure 23-2.

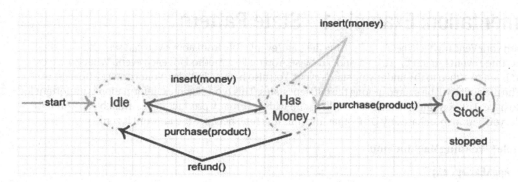

Figure 23-2. *Vending machine example*

You can convert this diagram into an event table. On the top are the states you need to create. On the left side are the events for each state. The table contents describe what should happen for each transition (a state and event pair).

Event/State	IdleState	HasMoneyState
Insert	Switches to *has money* state.	Add more money to the machine.
Refund	Tell user "no refund."	Give back all the money the user put into machine. Put the machine back into IdleState.
Purchase	Tell user they need to insert money before they can purchase something.	If product is available and user has entered enough money to purchase, then call deposit on Machine and set state to IdleState.

Example Structure

Figure 23-3 shows the structure.

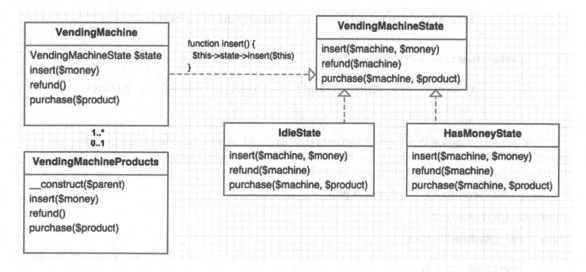

Figure 23-3. *Example structure*

Implementation: Example 1 - State Pattern

You start with your VendingMachine class. By using the state/event table from above you can see that a vending machine has three events: insert, refund, and purchase. You make a method for each event. What does each method do? It is a passthru to the underlying state's event. You also have to initialize your context with a list of products. The products will be shared among the different states. This type of context information is important for each state to have. The vending machine context keeps up with how many products it has available to purchase. For example, you cannot purchase any Dr. Pepper from this machine because the **amount** is zero.

app/Example1/VendingMachine.php

```php
namespace App\Example1;

class VendingMachine;
{
        protected $context;

        protected $products = [
                'Dr. Pepper' => ['amount' => 0, 'price' => 125],
                'Pepsi' => ['amount' => 1, 'price' => 125],
                'Mountain Dew' => ['amount' => 0, 'price' => 125],
        ];

        public function construct()
        {
                $this->context = new VendingMachineContext($this->products);
                $this->context->setState(new IdleState);
        }

        public function insert($money)
        {
                return $this->context->state()->insert($this->context, $money);
        }

        public function refund()
        {
                return $this->context->state()->refund($this->context);
        }

        public function purchase($product)
        {
                return $this->context->state()->purchase($this->context, $product
        }
}
```

Now let's take a look at VendingMachineContext. This class holds valuable information such as the current state, how much money has been inserted, how much money you currently have deposited, and information about your product prices and inventory.

app/Example1/VendingMachineContext.php

```php
namespace App\Example1;

class VendingMachineContext
{
        protected $state;
```

```php
        public $insertedMoney;
        public $totalMoney;
        public $products;

        public function __construct($products, $totalMoney = 0, $insertedMoney = 0)
        {
                $this->products = $products;
                $this->totalMoney = 0;
                $this->insertedMoney = 0;
        }

        public function state()
        {
                return $this->state;
        }

        public function setState(VendingMachineState $state)
        {
                $this->state = $state;
        }
}
```

This context class should be passed to each vending machine state. Here is your starting state, the IdleState.

app/Example1/IdleState.php

```php
namespace App\Example1;

class IdleState implements VendingMachineState
{
        public function insert($machine, $money)
        {
                $hasMoney = new HasMoneyState;
                $machine->setState($hasMoney);
                $hasMoney->insert($machine, $money);
        }

        public function refund($machine)
        {
                print "no refund available in idle state\n";
        }

        public function purchase($machine, $product)
        {
                print "you'll need to enter money to purchase $product\n";
        }
}
```

The insert actually shows a transition to the *has money* state. Notice what happens when you try to issue a refund or purchase event during the idle state. You still have to define what happens during these events. Sometimes an event does nothing (even if you made it print out some text).

203

> ℹ️ Had you found yourself needing lots of different events that never happen for a specific state, then you could have used an abstract class instead of an interface for VendingMachineState. Inside of the VendingMachineState you could have implemented empty methods for every event method. However, I like to specify each event even if it is empty. Even if it is more verbose, it seems cleaner to me.

Let's take a look at the next state, HasMoney.

app/Example1/HasMoneyState.php

```php
namespace App\Example1;

class HasMoneyState implements VendingMachineState
{
        public function insert($machine, $money)
        {
                if ($money < 0) throw new \Exception('You cannot insert negative money');

                print "you have inserted {$money} cents\n";

                $machine->insertedMoney += $money;
}

        public function refund($machine)
        {
                print "refunding {$machine->insertedMoney} cents\n";

                $machine->insertedMoney = 0;

                $machine->setState(new IdleState);
        }
```

When you are in the *has money* state and insert more money, you just keep adding to the insertedMoney property on the $machine. This is why context is important. Rather than use context, you could have put the $insertedMoney property inside of this HasMoneyState. That would have worked. However, there are other properties, such as $totalMoney and $products that are needed even once you transition to another state. Context communicates properties across states. You use those properties in the next event method: purchase.

app/Example1/HasMoneyState.php

```php
23    public function purchase($machine, $productName)
24    {
25            if ($machine->products[$productName]['amount'] < 1) {
26
27                    print "sorry, you are out of $productName, please choose another
28    product\n";
29                    return;
30            }
31
32            if ($machine->products[$productName]['price'] > $machine->insertedMoney) {
33
```

```
34
35              print "sorry, you need at least {$machine->products[$productName]
36    'price']}    to buy $productName\n";
37              return;
38          }
39
40          $machine->totalMoney += $machine->insertedMoney;
41          $machine->insertedMoney = 0;
42
43          print "[vending machine now has {$machine->totalMoney} cents]\n";
44          print "[vending machine spits out $productName]\n";
45
46          $machine->setState(new IdleState);
47    }
```

First, you make sure you have the chosen product in stock. Next, you check to make sure the user has inserted enough money. You can now move forward with the purchase by adding on insertedMoney to totalMoney. Lastly, you need to reset the state back to idle. Let's look at your vending machine in action!

app/example1.php

```
$machine = new \App\Example1\VendingMachine;

$machine->refund();
// no refund available in idle state

$machine->insert(50);
// you have inserted 50 cents

$machine->refund();
// refunding 50 cents

$machine->insert(100);
// you have inserted 100 cents

$machine->purchase('Mountain Dew');
// sorry, you are out of Mountain Dew, please choose another product

$machine->insert(25);
// you have inserted 25 cents

$machine->purchase('Dr. Pepper');
// sorry, you are out of Dr. Pepper, please choose another product

$machine->purchase('Pepsi');
// [vending machine now has 125 cents]
// [vending machine spits out Pepsi]

$machine->refund();       // because you  all hit
                          // that button after you
                          // buy a soda, right?
                          // no  refund  available  in  idle  state
```

Example 2 - Enter State Machines

In your next example, you will see a different type of pattern that has evolved from the state pattern. You can call it a state machine. State machines try to integrate part of the state pattern. You can see this state machine at https://github.com/definitely246/statemachine. The idea is that you create a reusable architecture for switching states of your client objects. There are many different ways to do this. One way is to abstract the state pattern out. The context no longer knows about states. The context only provides information and helper methods about itself. Let's take peek at your new Vending machine (context) class.

app/Example2/VendingMachine.php

```php
namespace App\Example2;

class VendingMachine
{
        protected $insertedMoney;

        protected $totalMoney;

        protected $products = [
                'Dr. Pepper'   => ['amount' => 0, 'price' => 125],
                'Pepsi'        => ['amount' => 1, 'price' => 125],
                'Mountain Dew' => ['amount' => 0, 'price' => 125],
        ];
        public function __construct($totalMoney = 0, $insertedMoney = 0)
        {
                $this->totalMoney = $totalMoney;
                $this->insertedMoney = $insertedMoney;
        }
        public function insertMoney($money)
        {
                $this->insertedMoney += $money;
        }
        public function insertedMoney()
        {
                return $this->insertedMoney;
        }
        public function refundMoney()
        {
                $refund = $this->insertedMoney;
                $this->insertedMoney = 0;

                return $refund;
        }
        public function products()
        {
                return $this->products;
        }
        public function numberOfRemaining($product)
        {
                return $this->products[$product]['amount'];
        }
}
```

```php
    public function priceOf($product)
    {
            return $this->products[$product]['price'];
    }

    public function purchase($product)
    {
            $this->totalMoney = $this->insertedMoney;
            $this->insertedMoney = 0;
            print "[vending machine now has {$this->totalMoney} cents]\n";

            print "[vending machine spits out $product]\n";
    }
}
```

Notice there is nothing about states in here. You only provide methods to do very specific things. If you call the purchase method on this class, it will purchase a product no matter the conditions surrounding this vending machine. This provides an easier and cleaner interface for your client since you no longer need to worry about states. It also means that you could add a state machine to an existing class at a random later time. So *if this* VendingMachine *class is no longer managing its internal state, then where is that being done*? For now, this code is left within example2.php but it could be further encapsulated within another (client) class.

app/example2.php

```php
$transitions = [
    [
            'event'  => 'insert',      // inserting money
            'from'   => 'idle',        // changes idle state
            'to'     => 'has money',   // to has money state
            'start'  => true,          // this is starting state
    ],
    [
            'event'  => 'insert',      // inserting more
            'from'   => 'has money',   // money is okay
            'to'     => 'has money',   // state does not change
    ],
    [
            'event'  => 'refund',      // allow idle to refund
            'from'   => 'idle',        // transition prints msg
            'to'     => 'idle',        // and state stays the
    ],
    [
            'event'  => 'refund',      // refunding when in
            'from'   => 'has money',   // has money state
            'to'     => 'idle',        // sets you back
    ],
    [
            'event'  => 'purchase',    // stops the fsm because
            'from'   => 'has money',   // all items have been
            'to'     => 'out of stock', // purchased and there is
            'stop'   => true,          // no more idle state
    ],
```

```
    [
                'event' => 'purchase',    // when you make it to this
                'from'  => 'has money',   // transition, you purchase item.
                'to'    => 'idle',        // order matters, see true above?
        ],
];
$vendingMachine = new \App\Example2\VendingMachine;

$machine = new \StateMachine\FSM($transitions, $vendingMachine, '\App\Example2\Transitions');
```

The upside to this approach is that you can easily manage your event transitions via this array. A state machine requires just two things: the transitions array and a context. The third parameter is a fully qualified namespace where the state machine can find transition classes. A transition class handles the transition from one event to another. You are required to define one transition class for every transition in the array. So how do you define a transition class? Let's walk through that now for the first transition in the array.

```
[
                'event' => 'insert',      // inserting money
                'from'  => 'idle',        // changes idle state
                'to'    => 'has money',   // to has money state
                'start' => true,          // this is starting state
],
```

The class name is generated automatically from the event, from and to attributes on this array. Thus, the class name you need to create should be called InsertChangesIdleToHasMoney. That reads well, right? This naming convention can be changed. You can visit the state machine docs on how to do that. So let's create your class.

app/Example2/InsertChangesIdleToHasMoney.php

```
namespace App\Example2;

class InsertChangesIdleToHasMoney
{
        public function allow($vendingMachine)
        {
                // always allow the user to insert money
                // when sitting around in the idle state
                return true;
        }

        public function handle($vendingMachine, $money)
        {
                print "inserting {$money} coins\n";

                return $vendingMachine->insertMoney($money);
        }
}
```

Each transition class needs two methods. The first method lets you know if you are even allowed to handle this method. This gives you the ability to ask the state machine if you can transition or not.

```
$machine->canInsert($money) // returns true because allow() returns
true
```

When you actually want to invoke this transition, you call the event name. In this case, the event name is insert.

```
$machine->insert($money) // invokes InsertChangesIdleToHasMoney::handle($vendingMachine,
$money);
```

After the handle method has been invoked by the state machine, the state machine switches from the IdleState to the HasMoney state automatically for you because you told it to do so in the $transitions array. There are five other transition classes defined. Please look at the source[2] if you'd like to see those in further detail. You are going to skip those here. Let's take a look at some more of example2.php for usage.

app/example2.php

```
$machine = new \StateMachine\FSM($transitions, $vendingMachine, '\App\Example2\Transitions');

print "machine state: [{$machine->state()}]\n";

$ourMoney = 300;

print "you have $ourMoney coins\n";

$ourMoney -= 125;

$machine->insert(125);

print "machine state: [{$machine->state()}]\n";

print "attempting to purchase Dr. Pepper\n";

// you can easily turn off exceptions
$machine->whiny = false;

if(! $machine->purchase('Dr.Pepper')) {
    print "asking machine for refund\n";

    $ourMoney += $machine->refund();
}
```

This code produces the output:

```
machine state: [idle]
you have 300 coins
inserting 125 coins
machine state: [has money]
attempting to purchase Dr. Pepper
you are out of Dr. Pepper, sorry...
asking machine for refund
```

---

[2]https://github.com/kdocki/larasign/tree/state/app/Example2/Transitions

You might have noticed the whiny property on the state machine. It toggles on and off exceptions. If whiny mode is true, then an exception will be thrown any time the state machine is asked to make an invalid transition. There is no purchase event handler when the state machine is in idle state. Had you not turned off whiny mode, the state machine would have thrown an exception. When whiny mode is off, it just returns false for invalid transitions. Next, you make purchase with whiny mode on (recommended).

app/example2.php

```
// put exception handling back on
$machine->whiny = true;

print "\nyou now have $ourMoney coins\n";

print "machine state: [{$machine->state()}]\n";

$ourMoney -= 100;

$machine->insert(100);

try {
    $machine->purchase('Pepsi');
} catch (\StateMachine\Exceptions\CannotTransitionForEvent $e) {
  ...
}

        print "----------------------------------------------\n";
        print "caught CannotTransitionForEvent exception\n";
        print "when whiny mode is active, you get exceptions\n";
        print "for invalid state transitions\n";
        print "----------------------------------------------\n";
}

if ($machine->canPurchase('Pepsi')) {
        $machine->purchase('Pepsi');
}

$ourMoney -= 25;

$machine->insert(25);

$machine->purchase('Pepsi');
```

output 2

```
you now have 300 coins
machine state: [idle]
inserting 100 coins
not enough money for Pepsi. machine needs 25 more coins.
----------------------------------------------
caught CannotTransitionForEvent exception
when whiny mode is active, you get exceptions
```

```
for invalid state transitions
----------------------------------------------
not enough money for Pepsi. machine needs 25 more coins.
inserting 25 coins
[vending machine now has 125 cents]
[vending machine spits out Pepsi]
```

Now that you've seen a purchase, let's see how the machine handles running out of products. This will call the StateMachineIsStopped exception because of the stop inside your transitions array. Once your state machine is stopped, it no longer handles any further transitions.

example2.php

```php
print "\nyou now have $ourMoney coins\n";

print "machine state: [{$machine->state()}]\n";

print "inserting 25 coins\n";

try {

        $machine->insert(25);          // throws StateMachineIsStopped exception
                                       // probably should handle
                                       // though, since a user w
                                       // you should just spit the
                                       // out and message the you
                                       // you are out of stock br
} catch (\StateMachine\Exceptions\StateMachineIsStopped $e) {
        print "----------------------------------------------\n";
        print "Caught the StopMachineIsStopped exception...\n";
        print "This means that the insert you just tried failed...\n";
        print "----------------------------------------------\n";
}
```

output 3

```
you now have 175 coins
machine state: [out of stock]
inserting 25 coins
-------------------------------------------
Caught the StopMachineIsStopped exception...
This means that the insert you just tried failed...
-------------------------------------------
```

You might have noticed that you added more transitions that your previous example. This is just to illustrate how straightforward it can be to create new transitions when using a state machine. This example does not look like the more traditional state pattern classes you had in your first example. The intent is the same, though. Keep in mind that your client in this example is spread out over example2.php. You could easily add your client class that looks like this:

example2 client

```php
class VendingMachineClient extends \StateMachine\FSM
{
```

```
        protected $transitions = [
                // transitions listed here ...
        ];
        public function __construct()
        {
                parent::__construct($this->transitions, new VendingMachine,
                '\App\Example2\Transitions');
        }
}
```

The problem with this state machine approach is that it is *magical*. You can't deduce the public methods on VendingMachineClient without knowing how the finite state machine works. You know that you can call the events found inside of the transitions array. That is because there is a magic call method inside the FSM that makes all that happen. However, it isn't obvious to any newcomers. Someone seeing this class for the first time would probably be taken aback. There is reflection and magic method calls going on under the hood here. This doesn't mean it's a terrible design; it just means that you can do it a different way if you'd like a less implicit state machine. That brings you to your next example.

Example 3

The next approach makes use of traits. You stick the state back inside of the VendingMachine class. Here is what it looks like now:

app/Example3/VendingMachine.php

```
namespace App\Example3;

class VendingMachine extends \StateMachine\DefaultContext
{
        use \StateMachine\Stateful;

        protected $state = '\App\Example3\IdleState';

        protected $context = 'this';

        // the rest of this class looks the same as it did
        // in example 2 protected and is omitted to keep it short
```

Your vending machine still handles purchasing and products the same way it did for Example 2. The difference here is that you use a trait called Stateful, which allows you to call the underlying methods on your state auto-magically. It is a little less magical than the previous example because you can look at the trait and the methods available in each state class. Let's take a look at the IdleState and HasMoneyState classes.

app/Example3/IdleState.php

```
namespace App\Example3;

class IdleState implements State
{
        public function __construct(VendingMachine $machine)
        {
                $this->machine = $machine;
        }
```

```php
    public function insert($money)
    {
            $this->machine->insertMoney($money);
            $this->machine->setState('\App\Example3\HasMoneyState');
    }


    public function refund()
    {
            print "no refund available in idle state\n";
    }

    public function purchase($product)
    {
            print "you'll need to enter money to purchase $product\n";
    }
```

Next is the HasMoney state.

app/Example3/HasMoneyState.php

```php
class HasMoneyState implements State
{
        public function __construct($machine)
        {
                $this->machine = $machine;
        }

        public function insert($money)
        {
                if ($money < 0) throw new \Exception('You cannot insert negative money');
                $this->machine->insertMoney($money);
        }

        public function refund()
        {
                $this->machine->setState('\App\Example\IdleState');

                return $this->machine->refundMoney();
        }

        public function purchase($product)
        {
                if (! $this->machine->canPurchase($product)) {
                        return;
                }

                $this->machine->setState('Example3\IdleState');
                $this->machine->makePurchase($product);
        }
```

You might notice this looks more like the traditional state pattern. This approach offers more explicitness in your design of your vending machine. It looks cleanest to me. I'm not a huge fan of traits because they often get abused. I think in this case it works. Everyone has their own preference, though. I have provided three different approaches to the state pattern. Pick your poison. *Smile.*

Conclusion

At the start of this chapter I mentioned it is a *glove* pattern. Don't use it unless it fits. A downside to the state pattern is that it increases the number of classes to maintain. If you only have a couple of states and events within your design, it might not be worth the overhead. Rather than have multiple state classes, it might be easier to have a couple of conditional statements inside your client class.

The Gang of Four book mentions that if your states don't hold internal variables, you don't need to construct state classes over and over. You can reuse the same state classes. Some would see this approach as the flyweight pattern since you have *state* objects being reutilized. It is likely that reusing state objects is faster because you don't have to reconstruct them over and over. That doesn't make it a flyweight. The flyweight is about reducing memory footprint. You probably don't have millions of different state objects floating around. Reusing a couple of state classes doesn't mean less memory (as you saw in the flyweight chapter). Who am I to argue, though?

There is another related pattern that looks identical to the state pattern. It is called the strategy pattern. Both patterns use composition to modify internal behavior. The main difference is that strategy is intended for algorithms, not internal state. You probably wouldn't use the strategy pattern for a vending machine because vending machines are known to be in different states in real life. Although the code structure between the state and strategy pattern can look essentially the same, the intent differs. I haven't covered the strategy pattern yet, but that is the next chapter. Let's get to it!

CHAPTER 24

Strategy

```
$> git checkout strategy
```

Intent

Define a family of algorithms, encapsulate each one, and make them interchangeable. Strategy lets the algorithm vary independently from clients that use it.[1]

Applications

The strategy pattern is useful when you have algorithms that share the same public interface but work differently under the hood. The strategy pattern generally relies on composition to pass in the varying algorithms. The Laravel encryption[2] component uses the same methods to encrypt and decrypt messages. The underlying cipher algorithm can change, though. This is a loose implementation of the strategy pattern.

```
$crypt = Illuminate\Encryption\Encrypter('secret key', $cipher)
$encrypted = $crypt->encrypt('secret');
$decrypted = $crypt->decrypt($encrypted);
```

Notice how the Crypt keeps the same interface methods of encrypt and decrypt, yet the underlying behavior changes when you change ciphers. This example embodies the concept of the strategy pattern. The missing piece and the reason I said *loose implementation* is that in this example $cipher is a string, not a class.

Abstract Structure

- Context is the class that holds the strategy object. It is what the client will interact with. When the method() is called, it will call $strategy->algorithm(). Since this class uses composition, you can easily swap out strategy algorithms by changing the $strategy object. See Figure 24-1.

- Strategy is an abstract class or interface. It defines the common interface methods for all algorithms.

- ConcreteStrategy1/2 are different algorithm implementations of a strategy.

---

[1]*Design Patterns: Elements of Reusable Object-Oriented Software*, p. 349
[2]https://laravel.com/docs/master/encryption

© Kelt Dockins 2017
K. Dockins, *Design Patterns in PHP and Laravel*, DOI 10.1007/978-1-4842-2451-9_24

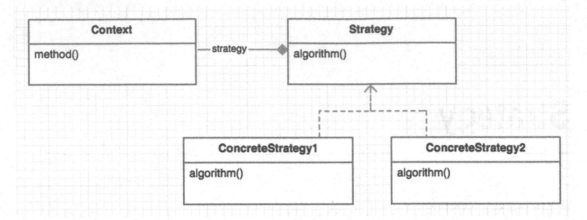

Figure 24-1. *Abstract structure*

Example

In this example, you are going to make a chicken. Not a tasty barbecue chicken. A noise-making chicken. Chickens make different noises. A rooster *crows*. A hen *clucks*. A chick *chirps*. Figure 4-2 shows the different noises made by chickens.

Figure 24-2. *Chicken noises*

Let's see what this Chicken class might look like if you use a giant switch statement for each type of chicken.

app/ChickenBeforePattern.php

namespace App;

class Chicken
```
{
        public function construct($noisetype)
        {
                $this->noisetype = $noisetype;
        }

        public function speaks()
        {
                switch ($this->noisetype) {
                        case 'hen':      return 'cluck, cluck';
                        case 'chick':    return 'chirp, chirp';
                        case 'rubber':   return 'squeek!';
                        case 'muted':    return '';
                        case 'rooster':  return 'cock-a-doodle-doo!';
                }

                return '';
        }

        public function scratch()
        {
                print 'scratches some dirt' . PHP_EOL;
        }
}
```

Every chicken speaks in a different way. This simple algorithm is about creating a noise for a given type of chicken. Similar to the Laravel Encrypter *class*, your noise-making algorithm outputs a string. The algorithm differentiates in the noise produced but your Chicken (context) class stays the same. Notice that all chickens scratch. You are going to use the strategy pattern to get rid of the switch statement found inside the speaks method.

Example Structure

Figure 24-3 shows the structure.

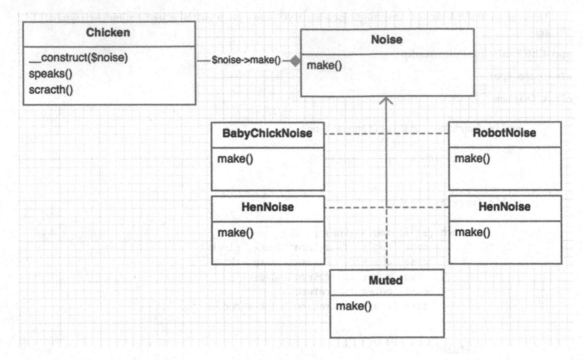

Figure 24-3. *Example structure*

Implementation

The first thing you will do is change your Chicken class to accept a noise-maker class.

app/Chicken.php

```
namespace App;

class Chicken
{
        public function __construct(Noises\Noise $noise)
        {
                $this->noise = $noise;
        }

        public function speaks()
        {
                print $this->noise->make();
        }

        public function scratch()
        {
                print 'scratches some dirt' . PHP_EOL;
        }
}
```

Now when a chicken speaks, he relies on his noise strategy to produce a sound. Any time you need to create a new noise, it is as simple as adding a new class. You no longer have to reopen the Chicken class. It is *closed*. This is the *open/closed* SOLID principle I talked about at the beginning of the book.

This brings us back to an important concept in programming, one you may already know well. Don't encapsulate all of the things. You only encapsulate things that will likely change in your application. Assume for a second that you are never going to add another type of chicken noise. In that case, the switch statement you saw earlier would probably be the better approach. Don't work too hard trying to solve problems that don't exist.

So how do you know if you should abstract some algorithm? Here is a tip. Do you find yourself reopening the same file to change something over and over? There is a high probability the class in that file is doing too much. Split that file into pieces. Use composition to split that file into different files. Use the strategy pattern if you've got an algorithm inside those files.

As you can see, the strategy pattern splits apart an algorithm using composition. However, just because you are using composition somewhere doesn't mean you are using the strategy pattern. Many patterns use composition. The intent of strategy is to make interchangeable algorithms. In this example, your algorithm is all about how to make noises. Granted, there isn't much to it but it is still an algorithm nonetheless.

app/Noises/BabyChickNoise.php

```php
namespace App\Noises;

class BabyChickNoise implements Noise
{
        public function make()
        {
                return "chirp, chrip\n";
        }
}
```

Want to see another noise implementation? Here is a Hen noise.

app/Noises/HenNoise.php

```php
namespace App\Noises;

class HenNoise implements Noise
{
        public function make()
        {
                return "cluck, cluck, BA-cawk!\n";
        }
}
```

If you'd like to see the others, please check out the noises in the repository[3]. Now let's take a look at how you use this class.

app/simulator.php

```php
$chicken = new \App\Chicken(new \App\Noises\BabyChickNoise);
$chicken->speaks();             // chirp, chirp

$chicken = new Chicken(new \App\Noises\HenNoise);
$chicken->speaks();             // cluck, cluck
```

---

[3]https://github.com/kdocki/larasign/tree/strategy/app/Noises

```
$chicken = new Chicken(new \App\Noises\RoosterNoise);
$chicken->speaks();          // cock-a-doodle-doo!!!

$chicken = new Chicken(new \App\Noises\RubberChickenNoise);
$chicken->speaks();          // squeeek!

$chicken = new Chicken(new \App\Noises\Muted);
$chicken->speaks();          //

$chicken->scratch();         // scratches some  dirt
```

Before your Chicken class had a $noisetype string and switch statement. Now you have more control by passing a Noise algorithm. This allows you to easily add new algorithms later down the road, too.

Conclusion

You've seen how the strategy pattern frees you from conditional statements. Each statement in the condition expresses its own behavior. This typically has the consequence of making code easier to understand. Another thing the strategy pattern allows you to do is pick which algorithm you want to use. One algorithm may have better performance 80% of the time. You can pick it 80% of the time. The other 20% of the time you may opt into the other, less-used algorithm.

There are a couple of drawbacks to the strategy pattern. The client must know about the different strategy objects. This extra complexity is minimal and can be negated with a service container auto-resolving the dependency. This drawback should not keep you from using the strategy pattern in Laravel.

The next drawback is that you are increasing the number of classes in your application. Is that really a problem, though? The more, the merrier, right? Earlier we discussed how you could have just kept the switch statement. *Sometimes* this is not a bad choice when the algorithm is simple enough. Adding more classes can add more complexity. The complexity lies in understanding how multiple classes are engineered to work together. However, the consequence of choosing not to use strategy pattern is a giant monolithic class that violates the open/closed principle.

CHAPTER 25

Template Method

```
$> git checkout template_method
```

Intent

Define the skeleton of an algorithm in an operation, deferring some steps to subclasses. The template method lets subclasses redefine certain steps of an algorithm without changing the algorithm's structure.[1]

Applications

The template method is useful when you have an algorithm that needs further instruction internally to run correctly. It fits well when an algorithm has steps, much like a cooking recipe. The *Head First Design Patterns* book uses an example of making different caffeinated drinks. Making a cup of tea is very much like making a cup of coffee[2]. A few steps differ, but for the most part you can reuse a lot of the steps. The template pattern is helpful when many steps are shared for variations of the same algorithm. The variation steps of the algorithm are defined in a child class.

Abstract Structure

- `AbstractAlgorithm` contains all the shared pieces between variations of the algorithm. The primitive methods that can be reused go here. See Figure 25-1.

- `ConcreteAlgorithm 1/2` contains overrides for missing steps of the abstract algorithm. The variation of the algorithm goes here.

---

[1]*Design Patterns: Elements of Reusable Object-Oriented Software*, p. 360
[2]*Head First Design Patterns, Chapter 8, p. 276*

© Kelt Dockins 2017
K. Dockins, *Design Patterns in PHP and Laravel*, DOI 10.1007/978-1-4842-2451-9_25

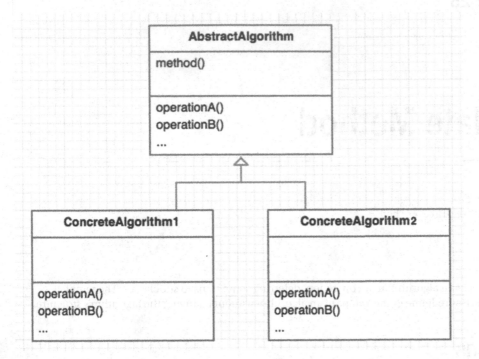

Figure 25-1. *Abstract structure*

Example

In this example, you will follow the steps a generic writer takes to create a document. These generic steps make a recipe (or algorithm) for any writer.

- Create a rough draft.

- Revise document after it fails the review process.

There are different types of writers. The type of writer you are depends on the type of document you produce. In this example, you will create software writers and magazine writers.

Example Structure

Figure 25-2 shows the structure.

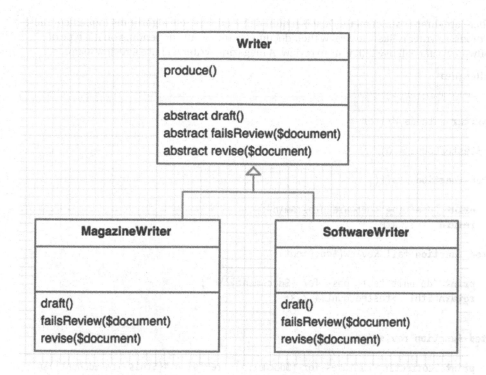

Figure 25-2. *Example structure*

Implementation

You start with your base abstract algorithm Writer. All writers can write. Writers typically follow the same recipe when writing. A writer will create a draft and keep revising the draft until it is good enough.

app/Writer.php

```php
namespace App;

abstract class Writer
{
        abstract protected function draft();
        abstract protected function failsReview($document);
        abstract protected function revise($document);

        public function write()
        {
                $document = $this->draft();

                while ($this->failsReview($document)) {
                        $document = $this->revise($document);
                }

                return $document;
        }
}
```

223

Notice that there are three abstract methods. It is required that all concrete algorithms implement these three abstract methods. A writer is likely to review their documents differently depending on the type of writer she is. A software writer will use unit tests to review. A magazine writer will use a review team.

app/SoftwareWriter.php

```php
namespace App;

class SoftwareWriter extends Writer
{
        public $testedCount = 0;

        protected function draft()
        {
                print "drafting software program\n";
                return "software";
        }
        protected function failsReview($document)
        {
                print "do unit tests pass for {$document}?\n";
                return $this->testedCount++ < 3;
        }

        protected function revise($document)
        {
                print "correcting mistakes for {$document} (revision #{$this->tesedCount})\n";
                return $document;
        }
}
```

Here is a magazine writer. Again, this different type of writer can have entirely different drafting, review, and revising steps.

app/MagazineWriter.php

```php
namespace App;

class MagazineWriter extends Writer
{
        protected function draft()
        {
                $document = "magazine";
                print "drafting {$document} document\n";
                return $document;
        }

        protected function failsReview($document)
        {
                print "reviewing {$document} document\n";
                return false;
        }

        protected function revise($document)
        {
                print "revising {$document} document\n";
                return $document;
        }
```

Running the simulator produces the following output.

app/simulator.php

```php
$writer = new \App\MagazineWriter;
$writer->write();
// drafting magazine document
// reviewing magazine document

$writer = new \App\SoftwareWriter;
$writer->write();
// drafting software program
// do unit tests pass for software?
// correcting mistakes for software (revision #1)
// do unit tests pass for software?
// correcting mistakes for software (revision #2)
// do unit tests pass for software?
// correcting mistakes for software (revision #3)
// do unit tests pass for software?
```

Conclusion

One of the major drawbacks to the template method is complexity over time. In reality, as you add more concrete algorithms, the pattern becomes more difficult to maintain. What if above you added another publishing step for copyrights?

```php
public function publish()
{
        $document = $this->draft();

        while ($this->failsReview($document)) {
                $document = $this->revise($document);
        }

        $this->copyright($document);
        return $document;
}
```

It might make sense to copyright a software program or magazine. However, what if you've got another concrete algorithm called HighschoolEssayWriter? A high school student doesn't need to copyright his essay document. This concrete algorithm would still need to override the abstract copyright method, though. This is a drawback to having a generic template that is in charge of your algorithms. It can be troublesome to branch off and do very specific customized things in your child algorithm classes. Adding the copyright method effects every subclass. You have to go change every class that inherits from the abstract Writer class. This means your abstract algorithm can become cluttered. This can be a pain in the neck to maintain, and many consider this a deal breaker.

Some people have complained about testing the base abstract class. This could be remedied by just creating a mock child class that inherits the abstract class.

Please read the blog article at http://tech.puredanger.com/2007/07/03/pattern-hatetemplate/ for more drawbacks of the template pattern. This guy gives some really good reasons to not use the template method pattern.

- It communicates intent poorly.

- It is difficult to compose functionality.

- It is difficult to comprehend program flow.

- It is difficult to maintain.

When you take a look at the structure of the template method pattern, it uses inheritance and no composition. I've already talked about how composition helps you keep from violating the SOLID principles. Long story short, use this pattern with extreme caution.

Visitor

```
$> git checkout visitor
```

Intent

Represent an operation to be performed on the elements of an object structure. Visitor lets you define a new operation without changing the classes of the elements on which it operates.[1]

Applications

This is probably one of the most complicated GoF patterns I've seen. The first time I stared at the UML diagram after a while I said, "hmm, wat[2]?" At its basic form, this pattern is all about extracting methods from semi-related or unrelated classes. When you do this, you no longer have to change or re*visit* (pun intended) the code. After reading more about this pattern I found out that some fancy-pants like to call it double dispatch[3].

What is double dispatch? Basically when you call a method, that method calls another method for you. So the method makes double the calls, hence the name. A language like C++ or Java allows you to overload methods[4]. You don't do method overloading in PHP. In PHP, you would need to use reflection at runtime for double dispatch. As you will find later, though, double dispatch is **not required** for the visitor pattern. I only list it here because other languages often implement the visitor pattern using double dispatch with method overloading.

Double Dispatch in Action

```
$dispatch->method(new Car);  // calls $dispatch->carMethod($car)
$dispatch->method(new Dog); // calls $dispatch->dogMethod($dog)
```

An analogy of the visitor pattern is a repairman who visits a house. The owner of the house can choose to accept or reject the repairman. If the owner called for a plumber but an electrician shows up, he could turn the electrician away. Assuming the repairman is accepted by the host, he can do his job. The homeowner doesn't need to know any details about plumbing. No longer is the homeowner involved at this point, save for a few questions and billing perhaps. The responsibilities of both the repairman and the homeowner are segmented. The inverse of the visitor pattern is the DIY (do-it-yourself) homeowner who can fix his own plumbing. The problem is there is only so much stuff a DIY homeowner can do without help from other parties.

---

[1]*Design Patterns: Elements of Reusable Object-Oriented Software*, p. 366
[2]www.destroyallsoftware.com/talks/wat
[3]http://en.wikipedia.org/wiki/Double_dispatch
[4]http://en.wikipedia.org/wiki/Function_overloading

© Kelt Dockins 2017
K. Dockins, *Design Patterns in PHP and Laravel*, DOI 10.1007/978-1-4842-2451-9_26

This "do everything yourself" problem exists in software, too. You don't want a giant class that does everything. Sometimes, however, real-life models can do a lot. Furthermore, real-life models will add more functionality and evolve. By using the visitor pattern you can add to your modeled class later on without reopening the class over and over, and violating the open/closed principle.

Abstract Structure

Figure 26-1 shows the structure.

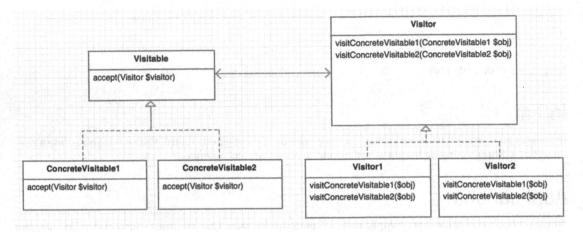

Figure 26-1. *Abstract structure*

Example

What do a woman and a chicken have in common? Feel free to tweet me your jokes to @kdocki[5] so I can tell them to my wife. In this example, both a woman and chicken can be poked. You can place the poke method inside each class.

```
class Chicken {
    public function poke() {   ...   }
    // ... other methods related to Chicken
}

class Woman
{
    public function poke() {   ...   }
    // ... other methods related to Wife
}
```

This works okay sometimes. However, what if you now want to add more methods? How about tickle, kiss, and chase? Eventually you keep adding operations into your classes and adding more and more responsibility to a giant monolithic class. Also, ask yourself, does a woman really need to know how to poke herself? Isn't that responsibility that should be placed elsewhere? In this example, you learned how to use the visitor pattern to add new operations to the Chicken and Woman models.

---

[5]https://twitter.com/kdocki

Example Structure

Figure 26-2 shows the structure.

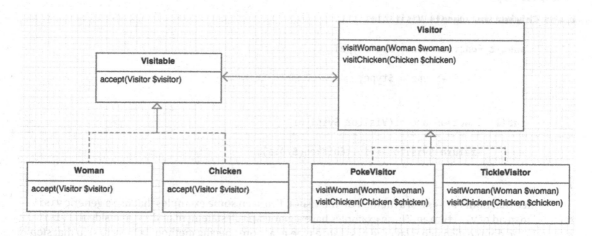

Figure 26-2. *Example structure*

Implementation

As seen in Figure 26-2, you abstract out operations into Visitor classes. Any class that can run these Visitor operations should implement Visitable. A Visitable can choose to accept or reject a new visitor.

app/Visitable.php

```php
namespace App;

interface Visitable
{
        public function accept(Visitor $visitor);
}
```

Your Visitables in this example are a Woman and a Chicken.

app/Woman.php

```php
namespace App;

class Woman implements Visitable
{
        public function __construct($name)
        {
                $this->name = $name;
        }

        public function accept(Visitor $visitor)
        {
                return $visitor->visitWoman($this);
        }
}
```

Don't forget the poultry!

app/Chicken.php

```php
namespace App;

class Chicken implements Visitable
{
        public function construct($type)
        {
                $this->type = $type;
        }

        public function accept(Visitor $visitor)
        {
                return $visitor->visitChicken($this);
        }
}
```

Notice that both classes call a method on the visitor. I've seen some examples that use a generic visit method instead of visitWoman. These examples have a giant switch statement and is_a[6] inside the visit method. The double dispatch relays the visitable type to a more specific method. I chose to skip that step because it is not necessary. You already know the type of visitable, so you can call it directly. You don't have method overloading in PHP, but you can simply name each method visit<VisitableType> to get around this limitation.

Next, look at Visitor.

app/Visitor.php

```php
namespace App;

interface Visitor
{
        function visitWoman(Woman $woman);
        function visitChicken(Chicken $chicken);
}
```

Every Visitor must know how to visit a Woman and Chicken. The poke visitor pokes a Woman and Chicken (Figure 26-3).

app/PokeVisitor.php

```php
namespace App;

class PokeVisitor implements Visitor
{
        public function visitWoman(Woman $woman)
        {
                print "the woman named {$woman->name} was poked\n";
        }

        public function visitChicken(Chicken $chicken)
        {
                print "the {$chicken->type} chicken was poked\n";
        }
}
```

---

[6]http://php.net/manual/en/function.is-a.php

CHAPTER 26 ■ VISITOR

Figure 26-3. Poking a chicken

Later you decide you want to add a tickle operation. This is as easy as creating a new visitor.

app/TickleVisitor.php

namespace App;

class TickleVisitor implements Visitor
```
{
        public function visitWoman(Woman $woman)
        {
                print "the woman named {$woman->name} was tickled\n";
        }
        public function visitChicken(Chicken $chicken)
        {
                print "the {$chicken->type} chicken was tickled\n";
        }
}
```

You could add more and more operations with new visitor classes. I'll leave the chase and kiss visitor operations up to you to implement. Now let's see how you would use your visitors and visitables.

app/simulator.php

```
$woman = new \App\Woman("Sally");
$woman->accept(new \App\PokeVisitor);
$woman->accept(new \App\TickleVisitor);

$chicken = new \App\Chicken('Dominecker');
$chicken->accept(new PokeVisitor);
$chicken->accept(new TickleVisitor);
```

231

Running this simulation outputs

```
the woman named Sally was poked
the woman named Sally was tickled
the Dominecker chicken was poked
the Dominecker chicken was tickled
```

One last thing to point out. Because PokeVisitor is a class, not a method, it can hold properties. These properties could be used to hold stateful information. This means the PokeVisitor has much more flexibility than a mere poke method would have placed inside of the Woman class.

Conclusion

The main drawback to visitor pattern is that every time you add a new Visitable type you have to create a new visit<NewType> operation in every Visitor class available. This can be mediated by using an abstract base class for Visitor instead of an interface. The base abstract class could implement a default for the method until a visitor class had a need to override the method. I've also seen some examples also use double dispatch in such a way for this problem. It is not recommended but I will show you how:

```
public function visit(Visitable $visitable)
{
        $className = get_class($visitable);
        $methodName = "visit{$className}";

        if (method_exists($this, "visit{$className}")) {
                return call_user_func_array([$this, "visit{$className}"] [$visitable]);
        }
}
```

The reason the above isn't recommended is because it adds complexity when you don't really need it. It is also more difficult to troubleshoot because it is using reflection. Solutions that use reflection can make debugging a stack trace more challenging.

Drawbacks aside, the visitor pattern makes adding new operations a cinch. This is assuming you don't add any new Visitable classes. However, if you are frequently adding new Visitable types, this pattern would be costly to maintain and give you mucho headaches.

An alternative to the visitor pattern is to use traits (mixins). It is often easier to mix in functionality to an existing class. Traits still have the drawback of adding more and more functionality to a class, though. However, this approach can be less confusing than implementing the visitor pattern to some developers. Having a generic double dispatch method called accept that you pass a visitor classes to can be daunting to newcomers on a project. This is because the accept method can do many different things depending on the type of visitor it receives. The genericness of accept is both its greatest weakness and strength.

CHAPTER 27

■ ■ ■

More Resources

Learning patterns is an endless battle. I've leveraged several different resources to help me during my research. I wanted to share these resources with you guys.

- Derek Banas YouTube videos of many patterns at www.youtube.com/playlist?list= PLF206E906175C7E07

- Blackwasp Gang of Four Patterns at http://blackwasp.co.uk/GofPatterns.aspx

- *Design Patterns: Elements of Reusable Object-Oriented Software* at www.amazon.com/ Design-Patterns-Elements-Reusable-Object-Oriented-ebook/dp/B000SEIBB8

- *Head First Design Patterns* at www.amazon.com/Head-First-Design-Patterns-Freeman/dp/0596007124

© Kelt Dockins 2017
K. Dockins, *Design Patterns in PHP and Laravel*, DOI 10.1007/978-1-4842-2451-9_27

Index

Get the eBook for only $4.99!

Why limit yourself?

Now you can take the weightless companion with you wherever you go and access your content on your PC, phone, tablet, or reader.

Since you've purchased this print book, we are happy to offer you the eBook for just $4.99.

Convenient and fully searchable, the PDF version enables you to easily find and copy code—or perform examples by quickly toggling between instructions and applications.

To learn more, go to http://www.apress.com/us/shop/companion or contact support@apress.com.

Printed in the United States
By Bookmasters